THIN PLACES

An Evangelical Journey into
Celtic Christianity

THIN PLACES

An Evangelical Journey into
Celtic Christianity

Tracy Balzer

LEAFWOOD
PUBLISHERS

an imprint of Abilene Christian University Press

THIN PLACES

An Evangelical Journey into Celtic Christianity

LEAFWOOD
P U B L I S H E R S
an imprint of Abilene Christian University Press

Copyright 2007 by Tracy Balzer

ISBN 978-0-89112-513-6

Printed in the United States of America

Scripture quotations, unless otherwise noted, are from The Holy Bible,
New International Version. Copyright 1984, International Bible Society.
Used by permission of Zondervan Publishers.

Cover design by Rick Gibson

Leafwood Publishers is an imprint of
Abilene Christian University Press
ACU Box 29138
Abilene, Texas 79699
1-877-816-4455 toll free

For current information about all Leafwood titles, visit our website:
www.leafwoodpublishers.com

To Cary, Kelsey and Langley,
my beloved fellow travelers

Contents

Acknowledgements

I would like to thank a few friends who've been a great encourage-ment and help on this journey: to Scot McKnight and Patty Kirk for their very fine editorial suggestions; to my sister, Wendy Rocker, for her willing-ness to read the roughest of drafts; to the Writing Women of John Brown University—Gloria Gale, Carli Conklin, Shelley Noyes, Robbie Castleman, Carrie Oliver, and Patty Kirk—for their enthusiastic and creative support; and to the many students and staff at John Brown University who have traveled with me to the British Isles and share my love for the rich Celtic heritage that is there. Also, humble thanks to my editor, Leonard Allen, for his professional guidance. And finally, love and gratitude to my family for their patience and encouragement, and for making me many cups of Irish tea as I wrote.

Preface

A wise person once said that the deepest need of the human heart is to love and be loved in return. As Christians, we believe that kind of love originates in the heart of God. He made the very first man and woman with the capacity to both love him and receive his love for them. Today we resonate with this reciprocal love, recognizing that it is what we need to live fully, deeply, sacrificially.

However, we no longer walk with God in Eden, enjoying easy conversation in the cool of the day. The distractions and preoccupations available to us in a fallen world draw us away from that kind of holy intimacy. We know intellectually that God is near, believing the promises of Scripture to be true: "I am with you always," Jesus said (Matt. 28:20). But the experience of it sometimes eludes us.

This book is written in hopes that its readers will find new ways of fostering intimacy with God—new ways that are not at all new, for they were practiced by Christians living in a distant time and a distant land.

In the year 563 A.D., 13 monks climbed into a small boat and sailed away from what is now Northern Ireland. They were in search of the ministry to which God had called them. Their leather boat landed on the shores of a tiny island in the western Hebrides of Scotland. This was Iona. Here they would found a new monastic community that would become one of the most influential centers of mission and learning of that time.

Today Iona stands as a symbolic testimony to the faith and work of these early Christian Celts. The ancient monastic dwellings no longer stand, but in their place is a magnificently restored Benedictine Abbey, formerly occupied by the members of a Benedictine monastery until the early 1200s when Viking raiders brutally forced its closure. TheAbbey is now under the care of Historic Scotland, while Iona Community, an ecumenical group of Christians, provides daily worship services for residents and visitors to the island. Through the combination of breathtaking scenery, historic Christian sites, and a regular pattern of worship, Iona becomes a holy place.

I have had the pleasure of visiting Iona a number of times, and am writing even now from there where my husband, Cary, and I have spent the week together. It is not, however, a journey of convenience. We flew from the United States to Glasgow, Scotland; took a train across the picturesque Western Highlands to the seaside town of Oban; boarded a ferry to the island of Mull where we then rode a bus across the island; and boarded a final small ferry that deposited us on Iona's white shores.

Iona is an insignificant dot on the map, an island only three and a half miles long by one mile wide. There are no grand attractions here, no shopping malls or theaters. Only the island's residents—right around 100 people—are allowed cars. Its population of sheep easily outnumbers the residents. Iona's landscape is rather stark with very few trees, and is surrounded by aquamarine water. Why do people from all over the world go to such effort to visit this remote place? *Why do I?*

Our journey through Celtic Christianity will provide the answer. The chapters that follow will begin with entries from my Iona journal, offering a personal glimpse into this sacred home of Celtic Christian history. They will help provide a context as we explore some of these helpful Celtic practices and attitudes. I hope that readers will gain a vicarious sense of the significance of this place for those faithful Christians who inhabited the island so long ago—but even more so for us today. "Visitors to Iona today are still captivated by the light, the colours of the rocks and stones, the wildness of the Atlantic waves and winds, the remoteness and perhaps most of all by a sense of the Spirit of God who has moved and inspired many generations of Christian people."[1] I can personally attest to the truth of this statement.

Following each Iona journal entry will be an introduction to these Celtic spiritual disciplines—their historical expression, as supported by various experts, and the practical ways these disciplines can be appropriated into our lives. Because they were clearly a people of poetic and regular prayer, each chapter will close with a distinctly Celtic blessing or invocation. Finally, each chapter of this book will include a Scripture passage intended to be used for meditation.

I pray you will be richly blessed as you embark on this journey, watching and learning from our ancient spiritual mothers and fathers in the British Isles. May you experience the nearness of God in new and transforming ways.

Deep peace of the Son of Peace,

Tracy Balzer
Isle of Iona, Scotland
April 2006

Introduction

One night when I was a very little girl, my grandmother tucked me into bed, helped me say my prayers, and I became aware of God. Not just the truth about God, but the reality of God, the living presence of God. Grandma's Roman Catholic faith had taught her many formal recited prayers. But this prayer was the same rote prayer that lots of other kids my age were probably praying that night:

> Now I lay me down to sleep,
> I pray the Lord my soul to keep,
> If I should die before I wake,
> I pray the Lord my soul to take.

—which I then followed with "God bless Mommy and Daddy" and every friend and relative I could think of. However, in the course of my request for the blessing of every living and not-living being I knew (I prayed then for my grandfather in heaven before I knew it was doctrinally controversial), it was I who became the one who was blessed, for a Presence made himself so real to my childish heart that it was as if heaven poured itself right into my bedroom.

We were visiting Grandma in North Dakota that summer, and during those hot, sticky days I would watch my grandmother and the rest of my Catholic relatives. I went to Mass with them, fascinated by worshipers dipping their fingers into holy water, making the sign of the cross over their bodies, and kneeling—not just sitting!—when they would say their prayers all together. I fingered Grandma's pretty blue rosary, with Jesus on the cross at the end of it. I listened to all that praying and prayed along as best I could, somehow aware that God himself was there in that holy place.

In the years that followed, my mother regularly took me and my younger brother and sister to church at the "Lutheran Church of the Holy Spirit." Here was another occasion for divine encounter, for in the same way that God became real to me through my grandmother's expression of

15

faith, the mystery of his Presence confronted me, young as I was, through sacrament and symbol.

I had my first communion at that Lutheran altar rail. Sacrament—"an outward sign of an inward reality"—utilized tangible elements to help make God real to me: thin styrofoam-like circles embossed with the cross, tiny cups of bitter wine. But there was more. My mother was on the "altar guild" at this church, so I often watched as she cut and sewed and glued and mended the pastor's vestments and the altar cloths, each embellished with all manner of symbols. Our church was, after all, called the "Church of the Holy Spirit," and the image of the white dove, appliquéd on Pastor Ellefson's stole, burned itself on my memory.

Then there was the Eternal Light, the red candle in the sanctuary that was so mysterious because it *never went out*. Every once in awhile I'd go along with my mother to the church late in the evening so she could retrieve some needed altar guild materials. I warily walked past the darkened sanctuary, and Something gripped my heart; that Eternal Light glowed red on the distant altar, and I felt that if I dared to speak aloud I would awaken the God that slumbered there.

I was only beginning the ecumenical trail of my spiritual formation. At the age of ten my best friend invited me to Vacation Bible School at her Christian Church, which was conveniently just down the street from my house. After two weeks of Bible stories, Bible crafts, and Bible verse memorization, I was ready to become a real Christian.

I prayed the "Sinner's Prayer" with sincerity. It all seemed like the right and natural thing for me to do. God and I were not strangers, after all. But the *Bible*—now that was foreign territory to me. Bibles weren't something that we toted with us to our Lutheran church services. Yet my VBS teachers at the Christian Church fairly oozed biblical conviction and enthusiasm, showing me that Scripture was God's way of speaking to me. I met Jesus through the words of God's Word.

I really learned to love those words, because they connected me to God in a whole new way. My grandmother had taught me about talking *to* God—but here was God talking *to me*! Even the holding of a Bible became a connecting point with God, especially because the only Bible we had in the house at that time seemed precious and even expensive: black leather cover, pages with gold edges, and the title of *Holy* Bible. One day my friend, the same one who originally invited me to come to VBS, showed me how cool it was to underline key passages in her Bible, and to even use different colored pens to do so. Well, if I was going to engage in that sort of religious behavior, there was only one thing I could do: get a Bible of my own.

That first Living Bible of mine underwent plenty of underlining, for sure. I find it no coincidence that my family's Bible—the black and gold one—was the *Holy* Bible, and therefore fairly untouchable. This Bible, my own Bible, was *Living*, and so my growing attachment to it was likewise.

I even heard God speak my own name in those pages. I read John 20, the story of the distraught Mary searching an empty tomb for her Lord, frantic to the point of thinking that the man talking with her is the gardener (of course it is really her Risen Jesus). Captivated, I reached the part where Jesus says her name—"Mary"—and I dissolved in tears.

I wasn't crying because I was sad that Jesus had to die, or because I was happy that he'd returned to life. I simply recognized how absolutely life-giving, life-transforming it must have been to be in the presence of Jesus and have him say Mary's name . . . to have him say *my* name. This story seized my heart, and I have known ever since that it is by direct encounter with the living Christ that I am sustained, transformed, and filled.

There were to be more ways to encounter God. In my junior high years I joined the youth group of Bethany Evangelical Free Church, and at first I was so ecstatic over being identified with them that I wore my green and white Bethany youth group t-shirt for about a week straight. This group was filled with really great, hilarious kids. A couple of guys had the Steve Martin comedy routine down pat, and when combined with some Monty Python schtick they had us rolling in the aisles of our big blue Bethany bus as we rambled to YFC nights or Christian concerts.

Most importantly, there was a genuine excitement in that group about God and it was contagious. They taught me about how to live out my faith as we sang together, witnessed to strangers, and enjoyed deep conversations around campfires. We pondered the mysteries of life, trying to get a feel for what God was wanting for us. We became burdened for those who did not know Jesus, and we began thinking seriously that maybe God could actually use us for some good in his world. We learned that Christians need to pray together and for each other. In this community God made himself ever clearer to me, showing me that my Christian faith was bigger than just me-and-Jesus. Pursuing God completely on my own would never be an option.

God had established a pattern with me, coaxing me along through prayer and worship, sacrament, Word, and community. When I chose to attend Seattle Pacific University, a Christian liberal arts college, I assumed that pattern would continue, and it did. I just didn't expect to be so profoundly introduced to another way of meeting God and enjoying his company. At SPU, I learned to love God not only with my heart, soul and strength, but also with my *mind*.

That mind was exercised to the hilt as I was confronted with all kinds of intellectual and spiritual predicaments. For example, was it possible to love God while studying astronomy? My professor apparently thought it was, for he enthusiastically expounded upon the scientific wonders of the cosmos, the depths of which could only be fully plumbed in the mind of God, the Creator of it all. He and my other professors across the disciplines regularly shared their enthusiasm, in and out of class, over the potential of the human mind to bring glory to God. And—wonder of wonders—somewhere in my junior year I found myself in their camp. By then I'd met Cary, my future husband who, as a straight-A student with seminary in his future, was also learning to love God with his mind.

I found my academic niche in the department of biblical and religious studies and became completely energized with the realization that the more I learn about God, the more there is to know. The Apostle Paul knew this was true: "Oh, the depth of the riches of the wisdom and knowledge of God! How unsearchable his judgments, and his paths beyond tracing out!" (Rom. 11:33).

As I learned to love God with my mind, allowing him to teach me and challenge me, I connected with him on a new level. Books became instruments of discipleship in God's hands as I discovered the delight of being tutored in faith through the works of great Christians. A.W. Tozer's *The Knowledge of the Holy*, Thomas a'Kempis' *Imitation of Christ*, Richard Foster's *Celebration of Discipline* were just a few titles in a long line of works that have fed my mind as well as my soul.

I became increasingly curious about thinking people who took their Christian commitment as seriously as I hoped to take it. Following our college graduation and wedding, Cary entered the ordination process in the Free Methodist Church. Soon after, we moved to Kentucky where Cary attended Asbury Theological Seminary. Suddenly we were surrounded by the very kinds of hearts and minds that intrigued me so.

In the midst of those seminary years I entered into my first spiritual direction relationship with a marvelous, godly woman named Margaret. She was greatly experienced in the art of prayer and spiritual direction, so I was thrilled when she agreed to take me on as a directee. We met every two weeks or so in her little office. That place became a sanctuary for me, because during our meetings, Margaret made it her goal to help me listen for the voice of God in my life. She asked me deep, probing questions about where I was seeing God at work, how he was challenging me, what was he showing me in his Word, and how was my prayer relationship with him. She helped me see all of these ways that God had met me and sustained me: through prayer, sacrament, the Word, community, the mind, and now through this very special relationship.

My friend Sally became another transmitter of God's grace to me. Sally's passion for God is unparalleled. While my relationship with Margaret was definitely one of director/directee, Sally and I like to think of each other as "soul friends." She is the kind of friend with whom there is no small talk. When we get together—which is too infrequent, as she lives in Washington State and I in Arkansas—Sally and I get right down to business. We dig into all manner of spiritual mystery: How are you seeing God in your world right now? (Sally always has great stories of seeing God's presence in her life: on the metro bus to work, in her dental patients, through her own recent heart surgery.) Have you read any great books lately? (We devour books by Dallas Willard, Henri Nouwen, Richard Foster, and some of the great saints of old.) How are you dealing with God's silence? (Each of us have had experiences of the seeming absence of God.) How do you see God forming himself in your children? (With two kids each we are learning together what it means to relinquish them into God's hands.) Yet our conversations are not so heavy as to be burdensome. On the contrary, sharing the journey of faith with Sally is sheer delight. I come away from my visits with Sally wanting more of Jesus in my life.

I think that while *people* are God's instrument of choice, *experiences* can also be an effective channel of God's presence and grace. Over a decade ago when Cary and I were in pastoral ministry in Washington State, I drove with Shelly, another good friend, up to beautiful Vancouver, B.C. We were going to Vancouver to attend a Silent Retreat—my first ever—that was to be led by author and speaker, Luci Shaw.

It proved to be a very clarifying weekend for me indeed. As Luci led us through long periods of silence and solitude, I sensed God drawing me into a new depth of connection with him. I learned then that this is called "contemplation": the prayerful loving of God and receiving his love through silence. Somehow this was not entirely new to me, but more of a recognition of something very basic to all of our souls, something that takes time to appreciate, something that can only be enjoyed if we are willing to stop talking and fretting for awhile.

In the course of the retreat our silence was intentionally broken now and then. Luci would lead us in corporate prayer and discussion. As I listened to this circle of virtual strangers—men and women, clerical and lay, Canadian and American—I found myself feeling like I'd come home, like this was family. They somehow spoke a language that resonated with the deepest parts of me. And Jesus sat in the midst of it all, symbolized by the candle Luci had purposefully lit. I felt like I could touch him—and I could, because he was present in Shelly and Luci and every person there. There was no denying it.

In the years since, I've grown in the conviction that silence is one of the greatest spiritual disciplines available to us. So now I teach college students about it, bringing them to an experience where they can attentively listen for the still, small voice of God. In terms of a life-giving connection with God, there's been nothing in my life to rival it.

With one possible exception.

On a Friday afternoon about six years ago I was browsing in the bookstore at the Christian university where I work as a campus minister when an unfamiliar title caught my eye. Nestled between various popular "how to" books on prayer was a title I hadn't seen before, *The Celtic Way of Prayer: The Recovery of the Religious Imagination,* by Esther deWaal. I snatched it up, not only because I'm always eager to read someone else's thoughts on prayer, but also because our university has significant connections to Ireland. Back then I at least knew that "Celtic"[1] had something to do with Ireland, even though a variety of thoughts and images also came to mind that day—from New Age pantheism (all things are God, particularly in nature), to barbaric behavior (including human sacrifice), to St. Patrick's Day parades, to a professional basketball team.

That weekend I devoured deWaal's book. It did indeed guide me into a much more accurate, historical definition of "Celtic." More importantly, it presented a doorway to a new-yet-old way of enjoying God. I was completely captivated by deWaal's presentation of an approach to faith that was so all-inclusive—a way of praying that actually made Paul's exhortation to "pray without ceasing" seem possible. This wasn't merely another technique or formula in order to be a better or more "spiritual" Christian. DeWaal demonstrated that the Christian Celts practiced an experiential, holistic expression of faith—a striking contrast to our modern lives which tend to be chopped up into parts: sacred and secular, church and work, worship and "real life." This ancient Celtic expression of faith presented me a lively and engaging way of what Brother Lawrence called "Practicing the Presence of God" while remaining biblically grounded and fiercely Trinitarian.

I was hooked.

Thus began my own Celtic journey, which has led me to many other authors who are committed to telling the Celtic Christian story. I've also traveled to the Celtic lands themselves: Northern Ireland, the Republic of Ireland, Scotland, and England (Wales is still on my wish list). The men and women of faith who lived in these intensely green, windswept lands have become mentors for me—people with names like Patrick, Columba, Brigid, Aidan—who couldn't have known that their lives would still matter over 1500 years after their earthly sojourn ended. The search for greater understanding of these incarnational, sacramental believers has become a passion for me, for I am a fellow pilgrim, trying to figure out what it means to live my life with a "deep consciousness of God" (1 Pet. 1:17, The Message).

The early Christian Celts have more than a few helpful suggestions for us. They include all of the ways that God has already connected with me throughout my life—prayer and worship, sacrament, Word, fellowship, intellect, friendship, silence—but delightfully enhanced by their unique Celtic voice. "The Gaelic race sees the hand of God in every place, in every time and in every thing . . . They have this sense of life being embraced on all sides by God."[2] They beckon us to join a life of freedom and joyful collaboration with God, where the holy presence of God himself can be easily accessed and enjoyed in particular places and experiences. *Doesn't that kind of life sound appealing?*

If so, come join me on this Celtic journey. He is calling us to meet him in the thin places.

One

THIN PLACES

From Earth to Heaven

Iona Journal

Tonight Cary and I attended the evening worship service at Iona Abbey. I have loved closing every day by going to these services. Each night at about 8:50 we hear the Abbey chimes calling us to worship. They help me think about God even before I walk in the sanctuary, reminding me that this abbey, this island, is not just another tourist attraction, but a sacred place.

Iona's Abbey is grey and gothic and stands alone on the eastern edge of Iona, with only a sheep pasture and the turquoise water of the Sound of Iona between it and the Isle of Mull, one of the larger in the family of islands called the Western Hebrides of Scotland. There is an ongoing restoration effort in the Abbey tower. Last time I was here on Iona, just three years ago, there was a great sheet of green plastic wrapped round the tower with scaffolding clearly visible. This time the plastic is gone, but the scaffolds are still in place. It strikes me as a good metaphor for the hundreds of pilgrims who come to Iona: we are new creatures in Christ, but there always seems to be more work to be done.

The two of us entered through the heavy, creaking wooden doors, and walked into the stone sanctuary, now warm and glowing with the light of many candles, the worship leader's call to worship echoing through the sanctuary as he sang. One thing I especially love about attending these services each night is seeing the now familiar faces of fellow travelers—those who were with us on today's boat trip to the island of Staffa, some who are staying at our hotel, others we greeted on the walk to North Beach. A few rows in front of us sat a couple we had traded cameras with earlier to take pictures of each other by the shore. Tourists have become worshipers.

Tonight's scripture happens to be my favorite of all the gospel stories, the account of Mary Magdalene meeting the newly risen Jesus at the empty tomb in John 20. Here on Iona it is just a few days after Easter, so the passage is a fitting choice. On Easter Sunday, Cary and I worshiped in Glasgow with the congregation of an historic church. The pastor spoke on this passage then, too, and I loved hearing the reader that morning present the story in her rolling Scottish brogue: "Mee—r-r-r—ee," she read, and continued describing Mary's instant recognition of her Lord at the mention of her name. Tonight, the woman presiding over the service in Iona Abbey read the account in the most exquisite English accent. It was music to my American ears.

I love this passage because Mary's encounter with Jesus was one of deep intimacy and friendship. The kind of intimacy we all long for and for which we are made. When Mary's eyes are opened to the reality of the living Jesus standing before her, a powerful connection takes place. In an instant, she once again knows and is known.

I can't help but reflect upon the many ways I fail to recognize the face and voice of Jesus in my own life. Like Mary, I find myself frantic or distraught, stressed and uptight, or sad and overwhelmed. My vision is too often clouded by my own distress, my eyes are drawn elsewhere by distractions. I turn in upon myself and cannot see that Jesus is right before me, saying my name, bringing me back to what is the truest form of reality: living in the presence of God.

Worshipping in Iona Abbey, walking these ancient pathways, watching the rhythmic pattern of the ocean waves—these are some of the mysterious ways that Iona helps me to listen and to watch for Jesus. And when I do, I find that he is, as St. Patrick prayed, "beside me, before me, behind me, within me...." *Everywhere.*

*"I have seen you in the sanctuary
and beheld your power and your glory."*
Psalm 63:2

What makes a place sacred or holy? Is it the presence of religious symbolism? Or Gothic architecture? Is it incense and candles, or quiet music meant to stir the soul?

Perhaps sacred locations are made so because of human-divine encounters, such as Jacob's struggle with God:

> *That night Jacob got up and took his two wives, his two maid-servants and his eleven sons and crossed the ford of the Jabbok. After he had sent them across the stream, he sent over all his possessions. So Jacob was left alone, and a man wrestled with him till daybreak. When the man saw that he could not overpower him, he touched the socket of Jacob's hip so that his hip was wrenched as he wrestled with the man. Then the man said, "Let me go, for it is daybreak."*
>
> *But Jacob replied, "I will not let you go unless you bless me."*
>
> *The man asked him, "What is your name?"*
>
> *"Jacob," he answered.*
>
> *Then the man said, "Your name will no longer be Jacob, but Israel, because you have struggled with God and with men and have overcome."*
>
> *Jacob said, "Please tell me your name."*
>
> *But he replied, "Why do you ask my name?" Then he blessed him there.*
>
> *So Jacob called the place Peniel, saying, "It is because I saw God face to face, and yet my life was spared." (Gen. 32: 22-30)*

Or they are made sacred by divine deliverance:

The men of Israel rushed out of Mizpah and pursued the
Philistines, slaughtering them along the way to a point below
Beth Car.
    Then Samuel took a stone and set it up between Mizpah
and Shen. He named it Ebenezer, saying, "Thus far has the LORD
helped us." So the Philistincs were subdued and did not invade
Israelite territory again. (1 Sam. 7:11-13)

Can a battlefield be a holy place? Samuel believed it was, enough so that he wanted that place to be remembered as such, a place where God himself came and helped in a spectacular way.

The earliest pagan Celts were profoundly aware of the spiritual world. Even before they came to know the one true God of the universe, they had an understanding of the unseen world, and perceived the reality of the spiritual world at every turn. Timothy Joyce explains that for the pre-Christian Celts, "[S]acred groves, rather than any building, were the places for worship and sacrifice. The oak tree, in particular, in its stature and strength, was the sign of the divine and its setting the site for religious ceremonies." He continues: "[The] mystical bent of the Celt was especially evident in the great love of creation and of all nature. This was not merely a romantic view of creation but a healthy respect for it, recognizing the dark side, the menace of nature's mighty powers as well as its beauty. This love of nature is central to Celtic Christianity and is the source of a wonderful heritage of nature poetry."[1]

The Celts that inhabited Ireland in the centuries surrounding the time of Christ had a name for particular geographical locations where the physical and spiritual came to touch each other in a special, almost tangible way. In their pagan, pantheistic spirituality, they believed there were places where the line between the spirit world and the physical world was "tissue-paper thin." These pagan Celts therefore referred to and revered such sites as "thin places."

Missionary to the Celts

It was into this pagan culture that Patrick came, clearly by divine appointment. Born in 387 A.D. into a noble British Christian family, Patrick did
not initially claim Christian faith. As a boy of only 16, he was kidnapped
by marauders from the west and taken to Ireland where he was sold into
slavery. For six years on the lush, green hills of what is now Northern
Ireland, Patrick endured a solitary existence as a shepherd, with only the
cows, sheep, and his own conscience to keep him company.

During these years of solitude Patrick returned to the God of his family. In his *Confessions* he tells the story:

> When I had come to Ireland I was tending herds every day
> and I used to pray many times during the day. More and more
> the love of God and reverence for him came to me. My faith
> increased and the spirit was stirred up so that in the course
> of a single day I would say as many as a hundred prayers, and
> almost as many in the night. This I did even when I was staying
> in the woods and on the mountain. Before dawn I used to be
> roused up to pray in snow or frost or rain. I never felt the worse
> for it; nor was I in any way lazy because, as I now realize the
> spirit was burning within me.[2]

Patrick eventually escaped his captors and found miraculous passage
back to his home in Britain. There he lived and served and ultimately became a priest. One night, as he slept, a vision came to him; an Irishman,
one of the men who had kept him captive, spoke to him.

> It was there one night I saw the vision of a man called
> Victor, who appeared to have come from Ireland with an un-
> limited number of letters. He gave me one of them and I read
> the opening words which were "The voice of the Irish." As I
> read the beginning of the letter I seemed at the same moment
> to hear the voice of those who were by the wood of Voclut
> which is near the Western Sea. They shouted with one voice:

"We ask you, holy boy, come and walk once more among us." I was cut to the heart and could read no more, and so I learned by experience. Thank God, after very many years the Lord answered their cry.[3]

Sensing that this was a divine directive, Patrick returned to the place of his captivity armed with the redemptive power of the Gospel.

One might suppose that Patrick and other Christian missionaries who so effectively evangelized Ireland would have made it their aim to completely eradicate the pagan concept of "thin places" and replace it with something, well . . . more *Christian*. But Patrick knew by his own experience that thin places were very real. The pagan understanding of it was simply misguided and incomplete. He himself had met the One True God on the Irish hillsides working for years as a slaving shepherd and had spoken with him daily, as if there were no separation between earth and heaven. Joseph Duffy's commentary is helpful in gaining a greater sense of the kinds of thin places Patrick experienced:

> Implicit in [Patrick's] account . . . is a positive atmosphere of stillness, whether in the woods or on the mountain or in the morning before dawn. This was more than the absence of human company; it was a stillness that enabled Patrick to listen to the emotions and memories that surfaced from his own depths. In this way he got in touch with his feelings of gratitude for being alive, for having survived the ordeal of the murderous attack on his father's house. In time these feelings enabled him to confront successfully his loneliness and isolation and physical hardship. The negative feelings were also strong and deep and never left him but somehow they became secondary to God's presence.[4]

Patrick's evangelistic strategy was not much different from St. Paul's own skillful presentation to a culture of very "spiritual" listeners:

> *Paul then stood up in the meeting of the Areopagus and said:*

"Men of Athens! I see that in every way you are very re-
ligious. For as I walked around and looked carefully at your
objects of worship, I even found an altar with this inscription:
TO AN UNKNOWN GOD. Now what you worship as something
unknown I am going to proclaim to you." (Acts 17:22-23)

Following Paul's example, Patrick simply and obediently poured corrective truth into the gaps of this pagan religion. And the pagan Celts
responded, readily embracing the Good News of Christ and easily trans-
lating their pagan beliefs into dynamic Christian expression. Thus, a thin
place was no longer a place where spirits, gods, and goddesses could be
seen or heard or felt through contact with the natural world. These holy
places now became recognized as sacred sites where the Holy Spirit of
God seemed as near as one's breath.[5]

Thin Places Today

Here we are given more than mere elaboration on Patrick's experience,
but wise guidance for our own. We are instructed that Celtic thin places
are not merely historical sites where something significant happened to
someone else once, long ago. A truly thin place is any environment that THIN
invites transformation in *us*, helping us as believers in Jesus to think and PLACES
see and understand as he does. Any place that creates a space and an Defined
atmosphere that inspires us to be honest before God and to listen to the
deep murmurings of his Spirit within us is thin.

We modern Christians can still visit the thin places of our early Celtic
fathers and mothers. Such sacred spaces are scattered throughout the
British Isles, concentrated mostly in Ireland and Scotland. The monastic
city of Glendalough in the Wicklow mountains on the southeastern coast
of Ireland is certainly considered to be a thin place by many. With its finely
preserved round tower, its cluster of ancient gravesites marked by Celtic
crosses, surrounded by the silent beauty of the Wicklow valley, Glendalough
has the makings of a truly thin place.

On our first Irish study trip with university students I enthusiastically planned a visit to Glendalough, having great visions of the spiritual retreat our students would enjoy there. Sadly, I hadn't been warned of the busloads of tourists that can descend upon its peaceful grounds on any given day. Glendalough certainly is a wonderful place to connect with God in meaningful ways. It is also a fantastic place to take photographs, so the presence of a great mass of tourists can "thicken"[6] it up pretty quickly.

Monasterboice is another significant site of a once flourishing monastic community. Founded by St. Buite, who died in 521 A.D., Monasterboice is on the east coast of the Republic of Ireland in County Louth, north of Dublin. What distinguishes this site is the presence of some of the finest and best preserved high crosses in all of Ireland, crosses that stand as great helps for meditation, as examples of fine medieval art, and as teaching tools as well. These crosses are intricately carved with illustrations of biblical stories and were most likely used as a sort of Christian totem pole to share the Gospel story with illiterate visitors to the monastery.

On our visit to Monasterboice, we allowed our students time for close examination of the crosses, followed by a quiet lunch on the cemetery lawn. Before leaving the site, we gathered around the great Western Cross, believed to have been created sometime around the ninth century. At seven meters high, it is believed to be the tallest of the surviving high crosses of Ireland. The Western Cross centrally features the crucified Christ, and also illustrates his baptism and Christ in the tomb. There are a number of Old Testament figures as well: Moses, Samson, Samuel, David and Goliath. We stood around that cross and held hands while we prayed prayers of thanksgiving for the great souls who had lived faithfully there a thousand years ago. Their faith was still visible here by what they left behind, these stone crosses a metaphor for the incredible staying power of the truth of the Gospel. The great span of years did not really separate us from our Celtic brothers, for it was truly a thin place.

Different from both Monasterboice and Glendalough (but equally as "thin") is Saul, the location of the very first church that St. Patrick established. History tells us that the pagan chieftain of that area, a man by the name of Dichu, was converted under Patrick's ministry, and promptly donated a barn for Patrick to use for worship services. It is memorialized by the rebuilt stone church that stands on the site in County Down, Northern Ireland. Saul is situated on a hill that is quintessentially Irish, for in all directions one can look out upon the patchwork fields of "forty shades of green," as the Irish proudly describe their lush landscape. Today the church building serves a living congregation, its stone walls just large enough to contain 100 or so worshipers.

My memories of this very thin place include celebrating the Eucharist with our students and the honor of having the local priest of the Church of Ireland (Anglican) lead and serve us that day. There was something quite powerful about gathering in that tiny church in the Irish countryside, knowing that the Lord's Supper had been celebrated by new believers at that very spot 1500 years ago. The dividing line between earth and heaven seemed thin, for we could sense a powerful kinship with that great cloud of Celtic witnesses that no doubt surrounded us that day.

Finally, the Isle of Iona itself is still known as one of the "thinnest" places, because so very much about it draws one's attention to God. The paternal presence of the restored Benedictine Abbey, where songs and prayers continue to be sung and said, and where twice-daily services welcome pilgrims from all parts of the world in unified, Christ-centered worship characterized by a distinctive Celtic gloss; the stone crosses that dot the eastern coastline, standing as sentinels lest anyone try to claim this island for any purpose other than its original intent; the bottle-green sea that gently massages the shore, baptizing the land over and over again with a sense of grace and redemption; even the ubiquitous sheep, ignorantly but contentedly grazing, unaware that they are padding around on saint-sanctified soil—are these the things that make Iona a thin place? Scottish poet Kenneth Steven eloquently asks a similar question in his poem entitled "Iona":

> *Is this place really nearer to God?*
> *Is the wall thin between our whispers*
> *And his listening? I only know*

The world grows less and less—
Here what matters is conquering the wind,
Coming home dryshod, getting the fire lit.
I am not sure whether there is no time here
Or more time, whether the light is stronger
Or just easier to see. That is why
I keep returning, thirsty, to this place
That is older than my understanding,
Younger than my broken spirit.[7]

Finding Our Own Thin Places

Perhaps a journey to the British Isles is not feasible. No matter! In fact, the very point I'm trying to make here is that thin places are all around us. While traveling to locations that are historically and spiritually significant can be a profoundly formative experience, I did not write this book merely to promote tourism. What we must try harder to grasp is this idea that Immanuel, "God with us," is absolutely and experientially true and that our spiritual ancestors in Celtic lands have a great deal to teach us in this pursuit. They knew the spiritual discipline of being alert and attentive to God's presence in all places.

I remember very clearly the first time I had the sense of being in a thin place. As a young girl growing up in Colorado, traveling one evening with my high school youth group to a mountain retreat, we found ourselves standing on the side of a windy mountain pass while our broken-down bus was being attended to. As we waited, my friends and I became aware of the inky-black sky, pierced with pinpoints of brilliant light—the kind of sky that is best appreciated in clear weather and high altitudes. We stood there, cocking our heads back in wonder, trying to take in the full scope of the sky. It was more than the general awe that most everyone experiences when confronted with the beauty of nature. This was a real moment of connection with God through the magnitude of his creation. There I stood at fifteen years of age, a mere dot on the face of the earth, yet

My thin places

I knew that I was loved and known by the Creator of all I could see. It was a transforming moment, genuinely changing the way I understood my identity before God and my place in the universe. That may seem rather grandiose, but the idea's not original with me. The psalmist articulated this epiphany quite well:

> *When I consider your heavens,*
> * the work of your fingers,*
> * the moon and the stars,*
> * which you have set in place,*
> *what is man that you are mindful of him,*
> * the son of man that you care for him? (Ps. 8:3, 4)*

Metaphor seems to be one of God's favorite ways of helping us experience his presence in thin places. About a decade ago, a group of wonderful praying friends of mine and I went to Cannon Beach, Oregon (which receives my vote as yet another among the thinnest places of the world) for a prayer retreat. I should admit that dwelling in a snug cabin on the Pacific Coast is my own personal recipe for bliss, so I was already quite content and ready to hear from God. But he had more to say to me beyond this blessing of place and surroundings.

As a group we had agreed to spend the better part of a day in silence and solitude. We began by asking the Lord to show us more of himself through some physical means. We determined to keep our eyes and ears open for the truth of God as revealed in Scripture and in nature and then be ready to come back together at the end of the day to share with each other.

If you have seen a postcard of Cannon Beach, you've seen its trademark image—the great monolith of Haystack Rock, which sits just off shore and characterizes the coast's dramatic landscape. It is easy for people of Christian faith to see that rock as a symbol of God himself, so it was natural for me to choose to meditate on the psalms that speak of him as our rock and our fortress. My Bible still displays my own small notation of "Cannon Beach, 1997" next to psalms 61 and 62. These truths were important for me to remember, as my family and I were in the midst of some disconcerting situations, most especially my husband's recent multiple sclerosis diagnosis. At that time, I was also hearing God call me deeper into the contemplative ministries of prayer, silence and solitude. It was clearly important for me to acknowledge God as my rock and my fortress because, unknown to me, the months to come would be laden with unexpected challenges.

However, it was in the shadow of that great rock that something very small spoke truth to me and provided me with an experience of God that made that stretch of beach truly thin. As I waited on God to show me more of himself, he also showed me more of *myself* through one of God's most curious creatures—the starfish. You see, when the tide is low, one can walk and climb all around the base of Haystack Rock and discover a myriad of fascinating plants and animals that make the rock their home. Tide pools are mini-aquariums full of anemone, limpets, barnacles, and snails of all sizes. To the side of the great rock itself the starfish cling, brilliantly tinted in orange, purple and red, unmoving against the tide. Why should they venture out into the churning sea, when the rock provides a perfect home? *Thank you, Lord*, I prayed that day as I explored this amusing collection of life forms. *That starfish is me. It* must *be me. Whatever comes, you are my rock, and I will cling to you.* My friends later gave me a silver starfish pendant as a reminder of this extraordinarily simple but profound word. That beach had become a very thin place.

others are thin places

Such connections with God are most often very simple indeed. His presence is rarely accompanied by cosmic fireworks; not many of us have burning bush encounters. Rather, we find that God's presence is most often more like the comfort we know when we are in the presence of a dear friend. Between ourselves and that friend there are no obstacles; only enough space for love to flow freely back and forth between us, either through words or through silence. This was, apparently, a common experience for the intensely spiritual Christian Celts, whose legacy of poetry and art confirm their sense of "the image of the natural world as a doorway to the sacred."[8]

Paul reminds us in his letter to the Romans that all of creation is a tangible, material witness to the invisible reality of God: "For since the creation of the world God's invisible qualities—his eternal power and divine nature—have been clearly seen, being understood from what has been made, so that men are without excuse" (Rom. 1:20). This verse claims that by looking closely at creation we can gain great insight into the Creator—into his character, his purposes, his ethic—his "invisible qualities." The early Celtic Christians knew what it was to seek God in all times and places, but particularly in those places that were completely free of man-made distractions. Perhaps this is one reason why Celtic monk and missionary Columba and his disciples chose windswept, virtually treeless Iona for their monastic settlement. It remains, even after many centuries, virtually unspoiled by human ambition. Columba wanted to insure that wherever he and his disciples landed to establish their ministry, he would not be able to see his beloved Ireland in the distance, lest his heart long to return there, tempting him to forsake his calling. From the shore of what is now known as St. Columba's Bay on the southern tip of Iona, Columba's heart was satisfied. To be able to see Ireland would be too great a distraction. It would make it too difficult for him to hear the voice of God.

I would also like to suggest that we can create our own environments of "thinness." It is true that the realities and responsibilities of life can make us feel tethered to the here and now, helpless in the effort to really get away from it all in search of thin places. Yet Jesus reminds us that the whole project is really very simple: a closet is all that is needed. We can look for such places in our homes—a corner, a comfortable chair, a room set aside to be sanctified as a thin place.

Living in a Thick World

A life characterized by regular, uninhibited connection with God takes practice and many seasons of what the classical faith writers call "consolation" (a sense of God's nearness) and "desolation" (a sense of his distance). You very well may be reading this right now with a greater sense of emptiness than fullness, a perception of distance between you and God rather than closeness. That feeling is altogether too familiar to me as well. I think every Christian, when being truthful, will admit struggling with Brother Lawrence's admonition to "Practice the Presence of God."[9] Our insides tighten up when we read Paul's challenge to "pray without ceasing." Too often the moments of our days go by without a thought of God. *Thin places?* You may be saying as you collapse into bed at the end of the day. *Are you kidding me?*

I find it extremely difficult to pay attention to God. There are too many voices calling for my attention. Too often I am over-committed and have too many obligations. I am tempted by the lure of consumerism and accumulation of things. I feel that the circumstances of my life are out of control. *There is just too much of everything.* It's as if I have spiritual claustrophobia. Everywhere in my life is a "thick place."

We have to make a particular effort here in order to clear out some space for God. Like Columba, we need to make sure that from where we stand we can no longer see our beloved Ireland, whatever that obstructive attachment may be. Our western lifestyle has filled us with so many things and so many activities that it becomes, as Henri Nouwen says, "absurd."[10] Many of these involvements can be good and helpful in and of themselves—it's just that the sum total can suffocate our souls. And into such a crowded "thick" existence, God will not push his way. He patiently waits until we make the intentional choice to do some housecleaning and make space for him, both in the literal sense of adjusting our physical environment, and in the soul-sense of bringing all our faculties to his attention. Visiting and re-visiting the thin places of our lives is one of the best ways to do this.

I recently had a vivid experience of the tug-of-war that is played between the demands of my life and my need for God. I was attending a conference of fellow campus ministers, set in the beautiful San Juan Islands in Washington State. It was an invigorating time of sharing ministry tips, listening to stories, laughing and worshiping together. Really great stuff. And it all took place just 100 yards from one of my favorite thin places: the beach. Yet during those five days, how many times did

[margin handwritten note:] "God won't push his way into our busy lives? ?

I actually get down to the beach? *Exactly twice.* I came all the way from land-locked Arkansas, greatly needing to meet God by the sea, and it almost didn't happen. What was going on? Busyness, most definitely. Days that were filled with enriching conversations and connections with colleagues who are true kindred spirits. So many good things. But even good things can keep me from the place of deepest connection with God.

Look for God in others Not Just Nature!

Of course God was right there with us in the busyness of our days. We definitely sensed his presence in life-giving ways. I simply didn't have the fortitude to say "no" to some of the scheduled events so that I could take the time to be fully attentive to God in the unique ways that thin plac-es allow. Finally on that last afternoon I stole away to the beach, when on my way I suddenly remembered that a group picture had been called for. Running back, I made it just in time to find my place in the picture, huffing and puffing as I pasted on a smile. *Good grief!* I didn't even make it down to the beach without the magnet of self-importance and obliga-tion pulling me right back into the thick of it! Of course, I was able to walk back down to the beach after picture time. But it makes me think about the moments I miss with God on a daily basis. It seems there's always something waiting to suck us back into the thick places of life, away from connection with God.

C. S. Lewis describes this phenomenon well:

> . . . the real problem of the Christian life comes where people do not usually look for it. It comes the very moment you wake up each morning. All your wishes and hopes for the day rush at you like wild animals. And the first job each morning consists simply in shoving them all back; in listening to that other voice, taking that other point of view, letting that other larger, stron-ger, quieter life come flowing in. And so on, all day. Standing back from all your natural fussings and frettings; coming in out of the wind.[11]

Conclusion

I have noticed that whenever I have the chance to share my enthusiasm for the faith expression of the Christianized Celts, the explanation of thin places evokes an instant sense of recognition among the listeners. It's almost as if an internal chime rings—*Aha! the ring of truth!* Smiles grace their lips ever so slightly and the slight nod of the head says, "Oh yes, I know exactly what you're talking about. I've been to a few thin places myself." I can also tell that they'd really like to go back.

For a physical location to be truly experienced as a thin place, it would seem that it mostly depends on us.

> *To go to Rome*
> *Is much of trouble, little of profit;*
> *The King whom thou seekest there,*
> *Unless thou bring Him with thee, thou wilt*
> *Not find.* [12]

This old poem reminds us that we cannot conjure up God. How many thousands of Muslim pilgrims flock to the city of Mecca each year, seeking divine approval and forgiveness? How many torn and desperate people sacrifice greatly to travel to Lourdes in the hopes that its holy waters will make them whole? These efforts reveal a true desire of the heart, but a misguided means of achieving that desire. If the Holy One does not reside and reign within me here at home in Arkansas, I should not presume to miraculously encounter him on Iona, or in church, or in the supermarket.

Seeing + knowing God in all places appears first

What makes a place holy? What makes a place truly thin? Before all else, the answer lies in our own internal landscape. Indeed, the first and best thin place must be our own souls. When, by the grace of God, that which has separated us from him has been removed, we can encounter the Holy One himself in freedom and friendship. Scripture tells us that the veil in the temple was literally torn in two when Jesus was crucified; we now have free access to the Holy of Holies. Our Christian forefathers and mothers in Celtic lands tell us that God is so very near that in some of his creation there is barely a film between him and us. Whether it be in a forest glade or on a starry night or in a quiet corner of a coffee shop, we have only to meet him there. If we truly want to be open to God and hope and seek for more of him in our lives, we can find him ever nearer and ever dearer in the thin places of our spiritual landscape.

Thin places merely amplify our sense of God's presence

Celtic Blessing

God be with thee in every pass,
Jesus be with thee on every hill,
Spirit be with thee on every stream,
        Headland and ridge and lawn;

Each sea and land, each moor and meadow,
Each lying down, each rising up,
In the trough of the waves, on the crest of the billows,
        Each step of the journey thou goest.[13]

Meditation: John 20:1-18

Early on the first day of the week, while it was still dark, Mary Magdalene went to the tomb and saw that the stone had been removed from the entrance. So she came running to Simon Peter and the other disciple, the one Jesus loved, and said, "They have taken the Lord out of the tomb, and we don't know where they have put him!"

So Peter and the other disciple started for the tomb. Both were running, but the other disciple outran Peter and reached the tomb first. He bent over and looked in at the strips of linen lying there but did not go in. Then Simon Peter, who was behind him, arrived and went into the tomb. He saw the strips of linen lying there, as well as the burial cloth that had been around Jesus' head. The cloth was folded up by itself, separate from the linen. Finally the other disciple, who had reached the tomb first, also went inside. He saw and believed. (They still did not understand from Scripture that Jesus had to rise from the dead.)

Then the disciples went back to their homes, but Mary stood outside the tomb crying. As she wept, she bent over to look into the tomb and saw two angels in white, seated where Jesus' body had been, one at the head and the other at the foot.

They asked her, "Woman, why are you crying?"

"They have taken my Lord away," she said, "and I don't know where they have put him." At this, she turned around and saw Jesus standing there, but she did not realize that it was Jesus.

"Woman," he said, "why are you crying? Who is it you are looking for?"

Thinking he was the gardener, she said, "Sir, if you have carried him away, tell me where you have put him, and I will get him."

Jesus said to her, "Mary."

She turned toward him and cried out in Aramaic, "Rabboni!" (which means Teacher).

Jesus said, "Do not hold on to me, for I have not yet returned to the Father. Go instead to my brothers and tell them, 'I am returning to my Father and your Father, to my God and your God.' "

Mary Magdalene went to the disciples with the news: "I have seen the Lord!" And she told them that he had said these things to her.

Reflection Questions

1. What is the thinnest place you've been to, and what made it so? What significant truth about God or yourself did you bring home from that place?

2. What thin place do you have access to right now? What obstacles are keeping you from that place?

3. What are the things that make your world "thick"? What can be done to minimize their influence?

4. What words describe your thoughts and feelings about being with God in a "thick" place?

5. What specific actions can you take to insure that you will pursue God in all the places (thick and thin) in your life?

Two

ANAMCHARA

From Soul to Soul

Iona Journal

I spent some time this morning at the nunnery ruins, just a short walk up the hill from our hotel. The ruins stand at the foot of a hill where cattle graze just to the west; on the north side were a flock of sheep that were terrifically vocal. It is quite entertaining to watch the new lambs jumping and skipping. (Who knew that lambs really did that? A fellow guest at our hotel joked with us—in a lovely British accent, of course—that it is said that there is one day in May when all the lambs corporately decide that it is time to stop jumping . . . and they do!) Lovely spring flowers grow in the middle of the nunnery ruins, clumps of yellow daffodils and sprinkles of something purple here and there. Modern benches have been placed about, giving visitors like me a place to stop for reflection and some blissful peace.

I walked into the section of ruins that was at one time a sanctuary, according to the map posted there. There are great arching windows, evidence that the ceiling of the sanctuary was quite high. Somehow it was not too difficult to imagine that community of women, living, working, praying together, even though it would have been almost 900 years ago. I sat down on a rocky ledge and thought about what it might have been like for a woman of faith and commitment at that time, and how she must have gained great comfort to come here with her sisters each morning, afternoon, and evening to pray together.

The nunnery ruins were a natural place for me to pray for the young women God has allowed me to mentor and guide in recent days: Kristen, Megan, Allison, Andrea and others. These college students are dear to me, and I never cease to be humbled that they consider me a guide for them. Do they realize that in the end, they actually guide me?

I had a dream the other night, I think in response to celebrating my birthday just a few days ago. In it I was talking with a woman whom I was guessing to be quite a bit older than me. She asked me how old I was. I replied, "Forty four . . . no, wait. I'm forty-five!" I asked her the same question, and she answered, "I'm thirty-five." I was shocked! It made me feel old—for just a second. I said to her, "Well, I guess I'm okay with being forty-five. In my thirties I felt I wasn't very well equipped to speak into another person's life. Now in my forties, I'm feeling a bit better prepared for that."

Yes . . . but just a bit!

There in the nunnery ruins on Iona, I sat on an old stone wall, opened the Scripture, and happened across Psalm 71:15: "My mouth will tell of your righteousness, of your salvation all day long, though I know not its measure." This verse encouraged me as I walked through those ruins, thinking of the young women God has dared entrust to me. It reminds me that I do not have to discern *all* of the mysteries of God and of life in order to help someone else on their journey. We tend to think of those who have been led into religious vocations—monks, pastors, missionaries, priests, the nuns who lived in this nunnery—as great wise sages who are perfectly equipped to model the spiritual life to others. But as I sat at the ruins, I imagined women living there who, though in a radically different time and culture, knew the same sense of inadequacy and insecurity that I often feel. They surely wondered, as I do at times, what they had to offer that could possibly draw others to God.

I prayed for "my girls" there at the nunnery, grateful for the opportunity to walk the journey of faith with them, and I recommitted to God that I will continue to tell them of his righteousness and salvation, "though I know not its measure." I'm fully aware that I am still a learner, too.

⌘

"He who walks with the wise grows wise;
but a companion of fools suffers harm."
Proverbs 13:20

As we continue on this Celtic journey, I hope a pattern, a recurring theme becomes clear—that the early Christian Celts were profoundly aware of the presence of God all around them. They enjoyed thin places where the spiritual realm of the heavenlies seemed so close they could reach out and touch it. Their lives were profoundly spiritual in the midst of a very earthy existence.

All this sounds quite wonderful—except that so many times we are completely stymied by what seems to be the absence of God. It is all well and good to speak in such glowing terms about sensing the presence of God, perhaps even hearing the voice of God. Yet that voice, as the prophet Elijah learned, is most often even quieter than a whisper. How can I ever hope to hear such a voice when my world is full of noise?

It would be easy to imagine the lives of our Celtic Christian predecessors as being spiritually idyllic (I'm quite certain I could hear God's voice better if I lived on an island!). With closer examination we find that while their circumstances were quite different than ours, these faithful Christians faced many of the same challenges that we do. They were diligent workers and were committed to the well-being of their communities. They had responsibilities at church. They raised families. Their zeal for God probably got them into trouble sometimes as they over-committed their time and talents. They likely struggled to distinguish the calling of God from what was merely an over-active sense of obligation. Like us, they were sometimes mystified by the silence of God.

They also did battle with their own sinful nature. New interest in the ancient Celts has emerged in recent decades, and some writings have painted Celtic faith with somewhat liberal strokes. We need to be clear that the early Celtic Christians were in no way soft on sin. The fallenness of the human condition was always metaphorically present to them through their own physical vulnerability to the harsh elements they were exposed to regularly in the British Isles. The reality of that weakness when applied to matters of the soul was experienced firsthand as they struggled to live together in peace and work together as a community of believers. They believed the Holy Scriptures when it says that none of us is righteous (Rom. 3:10) and that we all have fallen short of the glory of God (Rom. 3:23).

How did the Christian Celts weather the challenges that come to all believers? Reliable sources reveal that in times of good fortune and times of need, in dancing and in mourning, in the eternal gray of winter and the sparkling clarity of spring, each member of the Celtic community of faith had an *anamchara*—a friend and guide—to walk the journey of faith with them.

Anamchara ("ah-num-kah-ra") is Gaelic, the language of the Celtic lands, and when translated means "soul friend." This concept was distinctive in early Celtic Christianity, particularly in monastic life, where every monk was to be assigned to an older brother in the community, a soul friend, resulting in a relationship of utmost importance in the monastery. There is a well-known Celtic story in which St. Brigid (457-525), Abbess of the great monastery at Kildare, Ireland, once gave the advice that "a person without a soul friend is like a body without a head." In the Celtic way of thinking, having an *anamchara* was essential in one's life.

Celtic scholar and writer Edward Sellner says that "to be a soul friend is to provide a cell, a place of sanctuary to another where, through our acceptance, love, and hospitality, he or she can grow in wisdom, and both of us in depth."[1] Such a relationship "came to be closely associated in Christianity with ongoing transformation, a process of conversion-reconciliation that included frequent self-disclosure."[2] Ray Simpson explains:

> The "soul" in Celtic, as in biblical thinking, refers to the total self. It does not refer to a bit of a person, a spiritual bit, as in Greek thinking which splits the spiritual from the material. The "soul" refers to the whole personality: body, mind and spirit. The *anamchara* was a person with whom you could talk

through practical matters, reveal hidden intimacies, and break through the barriers of convention and egotism to an eternal unity of your soul.[3]

St. Patrick himself had a soul friend, a monk named Germanus in a monastery in Gaul (modern day France). The *Life of Patrick* states that during his time there with Germanus, Patrick "learned, loved, and treasured wholeheartedly knowledge, wisdom, purity, and every benefit to soul and spirit."[4] Surely Patrick's ultimate and profound influence in Ireland was partially due to the formative time he spent under Germanus' tutelage.

Origins

How did this relationship come to be so widely practiced among the early Celtic Christians? In the pagan tribes and clans that inhabited Ireland before Christianity was introduced, a social structure was in place that elevated certain gifted wise men and women and seers in the community: the Druids.

The very word "Druid" evokes an automatic, presupposed image among modern folk, particularly Christians. We quickly imagine the mysterious, hooded figure, communing with evil spirits and engaging in Satanic ritual. We are not altogether wrong, for there certainly were Druidic practices that would suggest a connection with dark forces. However, there is a bit more to be learned about this mysterious and powerful strand of pagan society:

> Tending to tradition, leading the clan in sacrifice, and guiding the communal decisions were the Druids. These mystery figures of the Celts have often been regarded as their priests, but they were more a combination of *philosopher, theologian, lawyer, judge, ambassador, scientist, and counselor.* Caesar wrote that these people trained for twenty years or more before being acknowledged as full Druids. They were the "magi," the astrologers of their people, reading the signs of nature and the heavens. . . . They taught in riddles, especially liking triads, thus

handing down the myths and values of the people. . . . They led prayers before battle. . . . They also presided at most marriage, divorce, and funeral rites. . . . In summary, *the Druids were at the center of Celtic life*, providing a structured office to embody the spiritual, mystical, earthly, and cultural values of a people otherwise united only by language and origin.[5]

The early Celts greatly valued the role of spiritual advisor, even in their pagan, misinformed state of belief. When the Irish world was converted to Christianity, the use of spiritual guides was not discontinued, revealing another pagan practice that was ultimately redeemed and transformed as Ireland was systematically converted to Christian faith.

In his book, *The Celtic Soul Friend*, Sellner points out the common ground between the Celtic saints—Patrick, Brigid, Columba, Ciaran, Kevin, Columbanus, to name a few—and the pagan Druids. The lives of these saints, as conveyed in the hagiographic[6] records, reveal that Christian saints and pagan Druids filled many of the same kinds of roles in the community.

> Though the early Christian legends often pit the Druids against the saints in their adult lives, the latter in many ways are portrayed as successors to the Druids and Druidesses, with the same gifts of prophecy and second sight. . . .Considering that some of the saints' most significant teachers were Druids and that they themselves took on similar tribal roles, it is obvious how much those saints treasured what they had learned from their mentors and incorporated that wisdom into their Christian theology and ministries. They did not abandon it because they could not; it was a spiritual inheritance engrained in their minds, hearts, and on the deepest unconscious level, their souls.[7]

The primary difference was that the Christian saints now performed this role for the glory of God.

Roles and Purpose

There are many ways the objective of preserving holiness and ministry was attained in this relationship. We will take a look at two important aspects of Celtic spiritual friendship: sanctuary and confession.

Sanctuary

The *anamchara* served as "a sanctuary for others, strong enough, like the beehive huts that cling to the cliffs of Skellig Michael,[8] to withstand the force of wind and waves, traumas and transitions . . . soul friendship is a sanctuary where the worst part of us can be acknowledged so that genuine change can begin to occur."[9] The *anamchara* was a skilled listener, a pastor, a friend who by his or her very nature and character communicated a sense of safety and trustworthiness. Stephen Lawhead illustrates the relationship between a young Irish monk and his *anamchara* in his historical novel, *Byzantium:*

> Crossing the yard, I proceeded to a small hut set a little apart from the abbot's lodge. There, I paused at the entrance to the cell and, pulling the oxhide covering aside, I tapped on the door. A moment later, Ruadh bade me enter. I pushed open the narrow door and stepped into a room aglow with candlelight. The air smelled of beeswax and honey. Ruadh was sitting in his chair with his bare toes almost touching the turf fire on the hearthstone at his feet. As I came to stand before him, he put aside the scroll he was reading and stood.
>
> "Sit with me, Aidan," he said, indicating a three-legged stool. "I will not keep you long from your rest."
>
> Ruadh, was, as I say, *secnab* of our community, second only to Abbot Fraoch in the monastic hierarchy. He was also my confessor and guide—my *anamcara* [sic], my soul friend, responsible for my health and progress. . . .
>
> Many and many were the times we had sat together in this simple hut, deep in conversation over a point of theology, or

unsnarling one of the numerous tangles in my wayward soul's knotted skein. I realized that this might be the last time I would sit with my soul friend.[10]

The image created by Lawhead invokes a feeling of familiarity, of compassion, of comfort, of security. In a variety of creative ways, the *anamchara* communicated this to the apprentice, assuring them that they were not alone on the journey of faith. In the centuries when Celtic Christianity prevailed in the British Isles, these spiritual friendships were commitments for life.

Another way of understanding this provision of sanctuary, of a safe place through soul friendship, is to consider expressions of hospitality. In the literal sense a monk might share a cell, like the one described above, with his *anamchara*. The two brothers would share a home together, though it was likely not much more than a tiny hut made of mud and sticks. The larger monastic communities also operated with a common understanding that strangers and pilgrims were always welcome for lodging, healing, instruction, and rest. This mentality surely inspired this traditional "Celtic Rune of Hospitality":

I saw a stranger yesterday;
I put food in the eating place,
Drink in the drinking place,
Music in the listening place;
And in the sacred name of the Triune God
He blessed myself and my house,
My cattle and my dear ones,
And the lark said in her song
Often, often, often,
Goes the Christ in a stranger's guise.[11]

The *anamchara* was one who would recognize the image of God in each person, treating each seeker as he would treat Christ himself, creating a haven where truth could be spoken in love.

Sadly, we are lacking such safe places today. Some of us do not feel we can be our truest selves, even among fellow Christians. We fear their criticism or worse, condemnation. We are afraid to voice our honest questions about God and faith. We hearken back to our younger days as students in school, afraid to raise our hand with a "stupid question." And when it comes to struggles—financial, marital, occupational, etc.—we may feel that a non-believer provides a safer place for us, fearing that fellow Christians would expect us to have our act together. Whether these perceptions are real or imagined, they are obstacles to honest faith nonetheless.

A few years ago Cary and I helped lead a retreat at our university. I brought along a treasure of mine to show the participants: a tiny sand dollar, no bigger than a quarter. This was a treasure because on the day I found it on the Oregon Coast, the only sand dollars I could find were broken ones. They had been full grown, about four inches across. But the seagulls had gotten to each one of them, cracking them open in the back and stealing the contents away. I told the students about walking the beach that day, wishing I could find a sand dollar that was in one piece. I even dared to pray about it—then withdrew my prayer, thinking it was silly. But sure enough, my eye eventually caught this tiny specimen, whole and undamaged, fragile and so vulnerable amidst all of the sand dollar carnage around it. I told the group I'd be happy for them to see it, to pass it around the room. But to please be very careful with it, because clearly it was very precious to me. *Please do not break my sand dollar.*

Each of us has something very precious, fragile, vulnerable inside of us that we would love to share with someone else—a husband, a wife, a sibling, a close friend. But what if that someone is careless with it? What if they crack it open, drop it, or worse, cruelly crush it? It feels too risky, so we keep that precious thing inside us, robbing ourselves and others of an opportunity for new insight and growth.

The Celtic *anamchara* would know how to lovingly handle that "sand dollar."

Confession

Providing a safe place that inspired confidence was critical, for another role the Celtic soul friend played was that of confessor. The *anamchara* was expected to provide accountability and correction to the young apprentice in faith.

' It was also the *anamchara's* role to assign appropriate disciplines to the penitent, not as punishment, but as further means to be trained in holiness. For example, if laziness was confessed, the *anamchara* might require the penitent to do another community member's work in addition to their own. If gluttony was confessed, fasting would be prescribed as penance, with the goal of learning moderation. When more grievous sins were confessed, the prescribed penance would be more serious.

Columba, or Columcille (Irish for "dove of the Church"[12]), is known as one of the three great saints of Ireland, along with Brigid and Patrick. A significant event in this saint's life was his penitential exile from Ireland assigned by his own *anamchara,* St. Molaise of Devenish Island. Columba was accused of copyright breach after allegedly copying a Psalter without proper permission, which led (though not really known how) to a bloody battle between Columba's tribe and the tribe of the king. While scholars debate how or even if these events were directly connected to Columba's exile, the historicity of his imposed exile cannot be disputed.

Prior to his exile, Columba was known as a believer of noble birth, deeply involved in pastoral and evangelistic ministry in the generation following Patrick. Columba founded numerous monasteries in Ireland that became widely known for excellence in teaching, spirituality and art. These centers of faith and learning produced exquisite expressions of faith, such as the great carved high crosses and illuminated copies of the Scriptures.

Columba's exile led him to Iona where he and his successors prepared many missionaries for evangelistic ministry in Great Britain and beyond to the continent, setting into motion the re-evangelization of territories that had been plunged into religious and social darkness by the fall of the Roman Empire. Columba's vision reignited the truth and it spread like wildfire.

Curing the Soul

The *anamchara*'s work, then, was "to apply the appropriate cure to the soul's disease," as Esther deWaal so aptly describes it. "Here is the work of the spiritual doctor curing the wounds of the soul, restoring what is weak to a complete state of health. Christ himself is, of course, the physician, but it is the soul-friend [sic] who has to impose an appropriate penance after the confession of sins."[13]

Those of us raised in the Protestant tradition might recoil at the idea of confessing our sins to someone else. Isn't God the only one who can pronounce that we are forgiven? It is true that no other human can grant forgiveness. But a soul friend can grant the *assurance* of forgiveness. The *anamchara's* voice and presence were tools God used to remind the penitent of the truth of absolution.

Another reason this practice of confession is all too rare today is simply that the very idea is completely intimidating, even though James tells us in his epistle that to do so leads to healing (James 5:16). None of us relish the idea of gazing at the dark places of our soul, particularly in the presence of another. However, in the Celtic tradition, "penance is thought of in a positive light, as making an act of dedication for love of God in order to overcome and leave behind the things that have hindered that love."[14] The pain of self-revelation was worth it.

A few years ago I invited my friend and colleague Sherry Bunge Mortenson to speak at the annual retreat for our female students. She spoke to them (and to me) about the "power of the secret." If our compulsions, our addictions, our warped conceptions are not brought out into the open, she urged, we are not able to receive the healing we so desperately need. Denial is a dangerous thing and is contrary to the truth, integrity, and freedom that is to mark the Christian life. Hiding behind an illusion of wholeness will not make the disease in a soul go away. Sherry implored us all to "break the secret" so that healing can begin.

To do so takes great courage. When mysterious symptoms surface in our physical bodies, doesn't it take courage to make the appointment to see the doctor? It is so much easier to ignore the issue, pretend it's not there, convince ourselves that it will take care of itself and go away. That simply will not happen if the issue is serious. The ailment that threatens us must be dealt with or even greater consequences will be suffered. We can just see, then, how deWaal's metaphor fits. We need a trustworthy confessor in our lives to help us detect the sin sickness from which we are suffering, and then get on with the treatment before the consequences reach overwhelming proportions.

The idea of revealing the raw realities of my deepest self is, I admit less than appealing. But to ignore the disintegration in my life is to invite spiritual implosion. I need to "break the secret." The early Christian Celts knew this to be true, so much so that to live life without an *anamchara* simply was not an option.

Scriptural Support

The concept of the soul friend was certainly not new with the Celts. As mentioned earlier, the role of the Druid naturally evolved into the *anamchara* once the former pagan communities converted to Christianity. Celtic monks were also inspired by the earlier desert tradition in Egypt— holy Christian mothers and fathers who lived ascetic lives in the desert and provided spiritual guidance for the pilgrims who would journey to visit them.[15] Prior to that, the example of Christ's disciples in the early church would have been of primary influence.

The Bible shows us a variety of soul friendships, each with its own unique character: Moses and Aaron, David and Jonathan, Ruth and Naomi, and the friendships of Jesus, James and John; Jesus and Mary, Martha and Lazarus of Bethany; and Jesus and Mary Magdalene. Each of these relationships demonstrates various aspects of soul friendship that lead to a greater love for God and sense of his presence.

The account of the two friends walking on the Emmaus road together (Luke 24:13-32) illustrates the role we can play in each other's lives as soul friends.

Now that same day two of them were going to a village called Emmaus, about seven miles from Jerusalem. They were talking with each other about everything that had happened. As they talked and discussed these things with each other, Jesus himself came up and walked along with them; but they were kept from recognizing him.

He asked them, "What are you discussing together as you walk along?"

They stood still, their faces downcast. One of them, named Cleopas, asked him, "Are you only a visitor to Jerusalem and do not know the things that have happened there in these days?"

"What things?" he asked.

"About Jesus of Nazareth," they replied. "The chief priests and our rulers handed him over to be sentenced to death, and they crucified him . . . In addition, some of our women amazed us. They went to the tomb early this morning but didn't find his body. They came and told us that they had seen a vision of angels, who said he was alive . . ."

He said to them, "How foolish you are, and how slow of heart to believe all that the prophets have spoken! Did not the Christ have to suffer these things and then enter his glory?" And beginning with Moses and all the Prophets, he explained to them what was said in all the Scriptures concerning himself. . . .

When he was at the table with them, he took bread, gave thanks, broke it and began to give it to them. Then their eyes were opened and they recognized him, and he disappeared from their sight. They asked each other, "Were not our hearts burning within us while he talked with us on the road and opened the Scriptures to us?"

Here we see, purely and simply, how these two friends helped each other recognize the presence of Jesus in their midst. I love this idea, because I have a lot of questions myself: *Where is Jesus in my life? What is he calling me to? Does he think about the various circumstances of my life?*

What is he saying that I am not hearing? I have found that these are questions I cannot answer on my own, for my own subjectivism and personal frailties tend to get in the way of seeing clearly. I need a soul friend to help me bring clarity to the murky waters of daily life.

A Model for Today

Though the circumstances of our lives are different from that of the early Christian Celts, the needs of our souls are the same. We need to approach our lives and work with an awareness of the presence of God in all things so that the result is a Christlike life that blesses others and honors God. The *anamchara* plays a critical role in that process.

Today we see this soul friend materialize in various ways in our Christian communities: as mentors, disciplers, pastoral counselors, spiritual friends. Another way the *anamchara* has been manifest throughout the centuries is the practice of spiritual direction.

Keith Anderson and Randy Reese co-authored a helpful book entitled *Spiritual Mentoring: A Guide for Seeking and Giving Direction*. The authors do a great service to those of us who are unfamiliar with the great contributions of historic Christians on this topic. They introduce their readers to Augustine, Aelred of Rievaulx, Julian of Norwich, Ignatius of Loyola, Teresa of Avila, John of the Cross, and Jeanne Guyon, all of whom lived and died before the year 1717. Yet their perspectives on life in the Spirit are remarkably fresh, and they have invaluable wisdom for us in the modern age regarding the practice of spiritual direction.

For example, Julian of Norwich made it her priority in providing spiritual direction to "point her mentorees toward the recognition of their unique voices for kingdom service."[16] Ignatius created spiritual exercises to call directees to higher levels of accountability. Teresa of Avila's specialty as a spiritual director was leading others in the stages of prayer and "greater responsiveness to the inner working of the Spirit."[17] Jeanne Guyon had this to say on the topic of spiritual direction:

It has been the habit of man throughout the ages to heal people by applying some remedy to the outward body when, in fact, the disease is deep inside. Why do converts remain basically unchanged despite so much effort? It is because those over them have dealt only with the outward matters of their lives. There is a better way: Go straight to the heart! Teach a believer to seek God within his own heart."[18]

Essentially, the role of the spiritual director is to ask thought-provoking questions of the directee that ultimately assist that person in listening to the voice of God in his or her life. Anderson and Reese suggest that among the myriad of such questions that could be asked, there are essentially three that the directee must be encouraged to consider: "Who is God?" "Who am I?" and "What am I to do with my life?"[18] These questions are always asked in humility before each other, before the Spirit of God, and before the Word of God.

Margaret was my first formal spiritual director. She was a fine Kentucky woman of prayer, a college educator, and a respected speaker and author on the spiritual life. When I first heard Margaret speak to a group of local women, I immediately recognized her as a kindred spirit and a woman I wanted to learn from. I had heard that part of her ministry was spiritual direction. So I simply asked her, by letter, to consider taking me on as a directee. She graciously accepted, and we began meeting together every couple of weeks to discover where God was working in my life.

At that time I was a young mother, struggling to figure out what a spiritual life looked like in the midst of caring for a newborn. I remember confiding to Margaret my frustration because I could not find time to pray and listen to God. Fatigue and the constant attention I was giving to my baby daughter seemed to sabotage my life with God. I clearly remember Margaret's life-giving words: "Honey, every minute with that sweet baby can be an act of prayer. When you're diapering that baby, let it be a time to pray and give thanks to God." What freedom that gave me! As an *anam-chara*, Margaret provided that safe place where I could be real about my inadequacies and concerns.

A spiritual director is also able to help us in discerning God's intentions for us. If I am confused about whether or not God is leading me in a particular direction, my director might ask me questions like, *Do you sense a call from God in this area? Does this decision bring you closer to God, or draw you away from God? What is your heart's desire? Is there some thread of interest that has run throughout your life?*[20]

What does spiritual direction look like on a practical level? There are some critical elements that need to be present in the relationship: the centrality of Christ, the authority of Scripture, the desire for transformation or sanctification. Beyond that, each of us is unique before God, and every direction relationship will be different. We need to ask ourselves what our own hopes and expectations of such a relationship would be.

Initially, anyone who desires this kind of relationship would be advised to begin by praying for the provision of an appropriate spiritual director. God may lead you to someone who is formally trained in the art of spiritual direction, a fellow church member, or someone down the street from you. God uses a wide variety of folks in this essential ministry.

What kind of person are we looking for? While praying for the provision of a director, we can be on the lookout for someone with the following qualities:

- a good listener—not only to people, but especially to God
- compassionate, non-critical—we are looking for that "safe place" that we see in the Celtic *anamchara*
- trustworthy—will keep our conversations confidential
- spiritually mature—not perfect, but growing and serious about following Christ
- Biblically literate—an easy familiarity with and respect for God's Word
- Humble—aware that it is the Holy Spirit who is actually the Director in the relationship

This might seem like a pretty tall order, and it can take some time to find such a person. In the search we need to remain open to God's creative answers to our prayers for a spiritual director. That person is often found in a place we least expect.

Being a Soul Friend for Someone Else

Our vision would be far too narrow if we only concerned ourselves with finding the director that is right for us. We also need to consider how God might be asking us to be a soul friend for another. Each of us are just a little farther down the road than someone else—someone who might really appreciate a fellow pilgrim to join on the journey.

If this suggestion causes undue anxiety, it's good to remember that it is indeed the Holy Spirit who is the true Director here. We cannot allow terminology to convince us that we are not qualified. If we return to the list of characteristics of a soul friend given above, we can ask ourselves, "Do I meet those criteria?" and discover, surprisingly, that God has equipped us to encourage others. In the Celtic world, the role of soul friend was most definitely not reserved solely for clergy. Lay people, both men and women, served in this esteemed role. Though a good working knowledge of theology was certainly helpful, the *anamchara* was not sought out primarily as one who dispenses theological information, but rather was one who walked the journey of faith and who was willing to help another do the same.

We sell ourselves short if we believe that we have no spiritual role to play in the life of another because we are not pastors, church leaders, or seminary students. Again, remember that the soul friend is not one who bestows knowledge and expertise on another, but is instead one who helps another *listen to the voice of God in their life*. It might be surprising to learn that in the typical spiritual direction session, the director, if he or she is taking the role seriously, actually says very little. The director's role is to listen to the directee, and simultaneously listen to the Spirit as he directs and illuminates. My friend, Jan Johnson, who has authored many helpful books on the topic of spiritual formation, gave me a prayer that I find myself praying regularly as I listen to my students: "Lord, help me

see her/his heart." The director must simultaneously listen to the directee
and the Holy Spirit.

Conclusion

A Celtic saint by the name of Morgan once wrote, "People cannot grow in
virtue on their own. We each need companions to guide and direct us on
the way of righteousness; without such companions we are liable to stray
from the firm path, and then sink into the mud of despair."[21] St. Comgall
of Bangor (7th century Ireland) stated in his Rule, "Though you may think
you are very solid it is not good to be your own guide."[22] We need the
anamchara in our lives to keep us connected to the Truth about God and
ourselves. Celtic saints Enda and Ciaran, both of Ireland, demonstrated
this through their relationship:

mentoring [handwritten margin note]

> After that Ciaran went to the island of Aran to commune
> with Enda. Both of them saw the same vision of a great fruit-
> ful tree growing beside a stream in the middle of Ireland. This
> tree protected the entire island, and its fruit crossed the sea
> that surrounded Ireland, and the birds of the world came to
> carry off some of that fruit. Ciaran turned to Enda and told him
> what he had seen, and Enda, in turn, said to him: 'The great
> tree which you saw is you, Ciaran, for you are great in the eyes
> of God and of men. All of Ireland will be sheltered by the grace
> that is in you, and many people will be fed by your fasting and
> prayers. So, go in the name of God to the center of Ireland, and
> found your church on the banks of a stream."[23]

If we feel removed from the voice of the Divine, it would be wise for us
to consider what Christians from earlier times have found helpful in their
pursuit of God. We do not need to invent something new, but should instead appropriate the wisdom of the past. Aelred of Rievaulx's[24] invitation
to embark on a journey of soul friendship is one we should take to heart:
"Here we are, you and I, and I hope a third is also present—Christ Himself.

Since no one else is here to disturb us, open your heart and let me hear what you have to say."[25]

Celtic Blessing

> *I am bending my knee*
> *In the eye of the Father who created me,*
> *In the eye of the Son who purchased me,*
> *In the eye of the Spirit who cleansed me,*
> > *In friendship and affection.*
> *Through Thine own Anointed One, O God,*
> *Bestow upon us fullness in our need,*
> > *Love towards God,*
> > *The affection of God,*
> > *The smile of God,*
> > *The wisdom of God,*
> > *The grace of God,*
> > *The fear of God,*
> > *And the will of God*
> *To do on the world of the Three,*
> *As angels and saints*
> *Do in heaven;*
> > *Each shade and light,*
> > *Each day and night,*
> > *Each time in kindness,*
> > *Give Thou us Thy Spirit.*[26]

Meditation: John 21:15-23

When they had finished eating, Jesus said to Simon Peter, "Simon son of John, do you truly love me more than these?"

"Yes, Lord," he said, "you know that I love you."

Jesus said, "Feed my lambs."

Again Jesus said, "Simon son of John, do you truly love me?"

He answered, "Yes, Lord, you know that I love you."

Jesus said, "Take care of my sheep."

The third time he said to him, "Simon son of John, do you love me?"

Peter was hurt because Jesus asked him the third time, "Do you love me?" He said, "Lord, you know all things; you know that I love you."

Jesus said, "Feed my sheep. I tell you the truth, when you were younger you dressed yourself and went where you wanted; but when you are old you will stretch out your hands, and someone else will dress you and lead you where you do not want to go." Jesus said this to indicate the kind of death by which Peter would glorify God. Then he said to him, "Follow me!"

Peter turned and saw that the disciple whom Jesus loved was following them. (This was the one who had leaned back against Jesus at the supper and had said, "Lord, who is going to betray you?") When Peter saw him, he asked, "Lord, what about him?"

Jesus answered, "If I want him to remain alive until I return, what is that to you? You must follow me." Because of this, the rumor spread among the brothers that this disciple would not die. But Jesus did not say that he would not die; he only said, "If I want him to remain alive until I return, what is that to you?"

Reflection Questions

1. Who have been soul friends to you? What was it about their presence in your life that drew you closer to God?

2. If there is an absence of soul friends in your life, what do you believe is the cause? What could you do (specifically) to seek out a soul friend?

3. Are you serving as a soul friend to someone else? If not, what are the obstacles that are keeping you from this ministry?

4. If you are serving as a soul friend—either formally, or informally—
   what can you do to make yourself even more fully available to God in
   this relationship?

THREE

PRAYER

From Ordinary to Extraordinary

Iona Journal

After this morning's service in the Abbey, I stayed behind, alone. I wanted, *needed* some time to be with God on my own—Cary went off elsewhere to do the same. I walked slowly around the sanctuary, looking at the various artifacts and taking time to really look at the magnificent Iona marble altar. Nothing in the Abbey is ostentatious. It is simple and streamlined in the attempt to create a sacred space.

A small corner to the right of the main sanctuary is designated as a place for private prayer. It provides a number of helps for pray-ers. One is a rough wooden cross onto which worshipers are allowed to pin small pieces of paper where they've written their prayers of thanksgiving or petition. One example, "Pray for my mum who is sick." Another, "Please save my brother Sean." On the other side of the prayer room I found a carefully organized notebook that contains prayer requests from the Iona Community. The book explains that the names listed are friends and members of the community around the world and it looked as though it is regularly updated.

I felt compelled to read through the names and their requests, and soon my heart felt heavy. So much suffering, and too often in multiple doses: losing a child, then discovering cancer; mental illness; MS . It is evidence of the Holy

Spirit's presence in my life that I can pray for people I will likely never meet this side of heaven, but pray for them I do.

I marveled that my appointed psalm for the day was Psalm 74, where I read these lines: "Do not hand over the life of your dove to the wild beasts; do not forget the lives of your afflicted people forever" (Ps. 74:19). This ancient prayer is perfectly designed for all the names that are in this prayer book here in the Iona Abbey, not only because of these folks afflicted with so many threatening "wild beasts," but the word "Iona," as I understand, is translated as "dove" from the Hebrew. So this verse in Psalms is my prayer for the "dove," the Iona community members who have asked for prayers.

> *"And pray in the Spirit on all occasions*
> *with all kinds of prayers and requests."*
> Ephesians 6:18

The word "prayer" can stir up all kinds of feelings—feelings of guilt ("I should pray more") to feelings of longing ("I want to pray more") to feelings of confusion ("I don't understand prayer") to feelings of consolation ("I feel closer to God when I pray") to feelings of desolation ("Why bother praying?"). But regardless of how I might feel about prayer on any given day, the fact remains: prayer is a pivotal connecting point in my ongoing relationship with God. If I'm not praying, I'm not really connecting.

The really good news is that there are so many ways we can pray. All of our experiences, actions, words, and various combinations thereof can be prayer. This is why it is indeed possible to pray without ceasing. The Apostle Paul is not telling me I must *talk* to God all the time;[1] he is, as Henri Nouwen suggests, telling me to "think, speak and live in the presence of God" all day.[2] The Celts learned this concept from the early desert Christians, who practiced *anamnesis*: the "conscious, prayerful

remembrance of God, the continuing sense of God's presence throughout the day as one works, prays, eats, talks, and rests."[3]

As I continue to learn about our Celtic Christian mothers and fathers,
it is this topic of prayer that inspires me the most. Not only did they celebrate the presence of God at all times and places, they were themselves
present to God. This is completely intriguing to me because I am not particularly interested in becoming an expert pray-er. Jesus had a few choice
words for those who paraded their prayer skills before those who cared
to pay attention. What I am interested in, rather, is becoming one who
perpetually lives in the presence of God, fully attentive to the reality of
his living, breathing Self that has condescended to be present to me. So
when I read that the Christians in the British Isles intentionally sought
God in moment-by-moment ordinary ways, my ears perk up and my
mind is quickened. This is something I want to learn more about.

Ancient Prayers

We can begin our investigation by looking at one of the most celebrated
Celtic prayers, "St. Patrick's Breastplate." It is a type of *lorica* (from the
Latin word for "breastplate"), a prayer of protection, and it gives us a number of clues about the Celtic philosophy of prayer and living life in the
presence of God. This prayer, while attributed to Patrick, was most likely
written by an unknown author several centuries after Patrick died. Yet
experts agree that it accurately reflects the theology and spirituality of the
real Patrick when measured against his autobiographical *Confessions.* "It
is a prayer enmeshed in the Trinity, in the immanence of a loving God, in
the goodness of a created world alive with the power of God."[4]

> *I arise today*
> *Through a mighty strength, the invocation of the Trinity,*
> *Through the belief in the threeness,*
> *Through confession of the oneness*
> *Of the Creator of Creation.*

I arise today
Through the strength of Christ's birth with his baptism,
Through the strength of his crucifixion with his burial,
Through the strength of his resurrection with his ascension,
Through the strength of his descent for the judgment of Doom.

I arise today
Through the strength of the love of Cherubim,
In obedience of angels,
In the service of archangels,
In hope of resurrection to meet with reward,
In prayers of patriarchs,
In predictions of prophets,
In preaching of apostles,
In faith of confessors,
In innocence of holy virgins,
In deeds of righteous men.

I arise today
Through the strength of heaven:
Light of sun,
Radiance of moon,
Splendor of fire,
Speed of lightning,
Swiftness of wind,
Depth of sea,
Stability of earth,
Firmness of rock.

I arise today
Through God's strength to pilot me:
God's might to uphold me,
God's wisdom to guide me,
God's eye to look before me,
God's ear to hear me,

God's word to speak for me,
God's hand to guard me,
God's way to lie before me,
God's shield to protect me,
God's host to save me
From snares of devils,
From temptations of vices,
From everyone who shall wish me ill,
Afar and anear,
Alone and in multitude.

I summon today all these powers between me and those evils,
Against every cruel merciless power that may oppose my body and
soul,
Against incantations of false prophets,
Against black laws of pagandom
Against false laws of heretics,
Against craft of idolatry,
Against spells of witches and smiths and wizards,
Against every knowledge that corrupts man's body and soul.

Christ to shield me today
Against poison, against burning,
Against drowning, against wounding,
So that there may come to me abundance of reward.
Christ with me, Christ before me, Christ behind me,
Christ in me, Christ beneath me, Christ above me,
Christ on my right, Christ on my left,
Christ when I lie down, Christ when I sit down, Christ when I arise,
Christ in the heart of every man who thinks of me,
Christ in the mouth of everyone who speaks of me,
Christ in every eye that sees me,
Christ in every ear that hears me.

I arise today
Through a mighty strength, the invocation of the Trinity,
Through belief in the threeness,
Through confession of the oneness,
Of the Creator of Creation.[5]

What a magnificent, celebratory, proclamation of faith! It's enough to change a person's perspective on St. Patrick's Day forever—which it did for me. I no longer dismiss the day as a useless excuse for rabble-rousing crowds to get drunk and wear green, though sadly, it will continue to do that. Now I'm compelled to thank God every March 17 for the profound impact St. Patrick and his contemporaries had on the spreading of the Gospel. I may not have an ounce of Irish blood in me, but I am a distant recipient of that great spiritual heritage.

Yet scholars and historians are careful to remind us that Patrick's prayer is not necessarily a template for *all* of the prayers prayed in the early Celtic Christian communities. In fact, if we were to name a template or pattern for prayer at that time, it would be the Psalms, for we know that in the highly influential monastic communities the Psalms were prayed throughout the hours of the day and night.

"Gaelic Songs"

A gentleman named Alexander Carmichael, himself a Scot living in the mid-1800s, collected and preserved a vast collection of original Gaelic hymns, prayers, and blessings—along with some rather superstitious charms, incantations, and omens—and compiled them in the classic work, the *Carmina Gadelica* (Latin for "Gaelic Songs"). These expressions of faith and culture have been passed down through generations ". . . by oral tradition as precious and intimate possessions, woven into the daily ceremony of rising, working, and going down to sleep. Through this ancient and powerful song, the inhabitants of the islands . . . sought protection and blessing, healing and strength, comfort and community."[6]

We can see the influence of prayers like Patrick's Breastplate in these Highland prayers. They share some important distinctions: repeated and overt reverence for the Trinity, as well as a threefold pattern in their prayers; a clear conviction that all activity can be consecrated and made holy for God's use, mirroring the monastic rhythm of work and prayer; the celebration of the immanence of Christ, and others that will be mentioned shortly. The Gaelic prayers of Carmichael's *Carmina Gadelica* show us that the unique characteristics of the ninth-century Breastplate were somehow sustained so that centuries later its definitive tone and emphases had been preserved.

In the *Life of St. Columba*—the hagiographic account written by Adomnan (624-704), ninth abbot of Iona—we are given other clues about what prayer might have been like for the earliest Christian Celts. Adomnan provides "rich descriptions of Columba's creative personality, his mystical connection with the land and sea, his love of learning, and his great capacity for friendship,"[7] as well as the picture of a man deeply and intimately devoted to God.

> Columba never could spend the space of even one hour without study, or prayer, or writing, or some other holy occupation. So incessantly was he engaged night and day in the unwearied exercise of fasting and watching, that the burden of each of these austere practices would seem beyond the power of all human endurance. And still in all these activities he was beloved by all for a holy joy shown continuously on his face, revealing the joy and gladness with which the Holy Spirit filled his inmost soul."[8]

Beccan mac Luidgech, a poet from Columba's monastic community, describes Columba "adoring God, nightly, daily, with hands outstretched, with splendid alms, with right actions."[9] Columba started a long thread of unceasing prayer that wove its way through history to the later 19th century Highland Christians. Now this great spiritual resource is available to us.

As we seek the Holy Spirit's guidance in reigniting our own life of prayer, these Celtic prayers—whether the prayers of the earliest Celts, or the prayers of the nineteenth century Highlanders—provide us with "new treasures as well as old" (Matt. 13:52).

Distinctions of the Lorica

How is it that we modern believers can be firm in our belief in the Trinitarian doctrine, yet are reluctant to invoke the name of the Trinity in our prayers and worship services? Loren Wilkinson comments on this phenomenon:

> Belief in the Trinity . . . is not unique to the Celtic Christian culture, of course. . . . Yet, as many have pointed out, a subtle deism is latent in much Western theology—some trace it to Augustine of northern Africa—which reinforces the oneness and otherness of God rather than God's intrinsic relatedness. Eastern Orthodoxy, with which the Celtic Christian vision often shares intriguing similarities, keeps this insight of interrelatedness of the Trinity (called the doctrine of *perichoresis*, or coinherence of the Trinity).[10]

Patrick's Breastplate reminds us of the unfathomable coexistence within the Godhead—threeness and oneness, all at the same time—and of the worthwhile practice of invoking that name, confessing our belief that God relates to us because God relates to Himself. We are part of this mysterious interconnectedness. Consider this beautiful Highland prayer, preserved in the *Carmina Gadelica*, that demonstrates the richness that is lost to us because we too easily brush past the living reality of the Trinity:

In name of Father,
In name of Son,
In name of Spirit,
Three in One:

Father cherish me,

Son cherish me,
Spirit cherish me,
Three all-kindly.

God make me holy,
Christ make me holy,
Spirit make me holy,
Three all-holy.
Three aid my hope,
Three aid my love,
Three aid mine eye,
And my knee from stumbling,
My knee from stumbling.[11]

Returning to the Breastplate, we see it also reveals its author's belief in the historicity of Christ's life, death, and resurrection, his acknowledgement of the world of the unseen, his celebration of creation as it reflects the glory of God, and his faith in God's ability to protect him from all manner of threats. Here we note that the Celts were indeed aware of the darkness that can be found in the world, that one of the consequences of the Fall is the sense that the world is not entirely safe. Threats that were visible as well as invisible drew them to prayer in humble recognition that we need holy protection from that which seeks to kill and destroy. As the centuries rolled by, this threat materialized in the form of Viking marauders who invaded the monastic cities of Scotland and Ireland, plundering their sacred relics and illuminated manuscripts, and sadly murdering many of the resident monks. In 806, Iona lost 68 monks in just one such raid.[12]

Protection was a common theme in Celtic Christianity as its influence moved across the British Isles and across the centuries. The Breastplate, as a *lorica* prayer, is "strongly biblical in inspiration and borrow(s) heavily from the passage in Ephesians 6:10-17 where Paul writes about putting on the whole armour of God."[13] Another protection prayer was the *caim*, in which the Celts would draw a circle in the earth around themselves with a finger as they prayed to the Trinity, entreating Father,

Son, and Holy Spirit to encircle and protect them.[14] Because there are so many of these protecting prayers, passed down many generations and finally recorded in the *Carmina Gadelica*, we have sufficient evidence that Celtic faith took the reality of sin and fallenness seriously. This is important today, particularly when the Christian Celts are improperly linked to new age mysticism, which clearly does not acknowledge the fallen nature of creation and humanity. The Christian Celts knew the power of sin, and therefore beseeched the Lord for protection against it; hence, the *lorica* prayers.

And finally we see in Patrick's prayer the poetic, hymn-like paean declaring the immanence of Christ, Immanuel, "God with us," in resounding agreement with the psalmist who proclaimed that God "hems" us in, "behind and before" (Ps 139:5). Throughout the Breastplate's celebration of the Presence we can hear the psalmist's rhetorical question, "Where can I go from your Spirit? Where can I flee from your presence?" (Ps. 139:7). The author of the *lorica* repeatedly gives the answer, a resounding confident proclamation that Christ is everywhere.

Such a viewpoint speaks directly to our modern tendency to divide life into categories: sacred and secular, Christian and non-Christian, heavenly and worldly, etc. In doing so, we inadvertently construct boundaries for the Holy Spirit, limiting the lengths to which we believe the Spirit can roam. For the Celt, no such division existed, because all of creation (though fallen and subject to sin) is God's domain. In the Celtic way of praying, God was invited to be present, to inhabit, to protect all manner of daily and ordinary activities.

As we consider this way of praying more closely, we may be tempted to dismiss these historic believers, thinking their lives were surely much simpler then. Less complicated, perhaps, but simpler? Not necessarily. If life was so simple for them, I hardly think they'd be praying those protection prayers with such fervor. No, these were a people who "have so much to do from dawn to dusk, from dark to dark that they had little time for long, formal prayers. Instead throughout the day they make each activity in turn the occasion for prayer, doing what has to be done carefully for its own sake but simultaneously making it into the occasion for prayer. Each thing in turn, however humble, however mundane, can be handed over to God or performed in partnership with the cooperation of the Trinity, saints and angels."[15] Again we see that not only was prayer offered in the most ordinary of moments, but that those ordinary moments were made extraordinary—they were sanctified and made holy by prayer. So it wasn't just that the line between sacred and secular was blurred, thereby neutralizing everything in a general sort of way. Rather, each action, each event, each task was made to be *holy*. All things, all tasks could be sanctified in worship to God.

The *Carmina Gadelica* is full of prayers and blessings that teach us new ways to enjoy God. There are journey prayers, blessings, thanks for food, night shielding, to name a few. Some may strike us as amusing, sometimes even superstitious: prayers for live creatures (including the gravedigger beetle and the sacred beetle), for the washing woman, and charms for healing (including thyroid gland, the uvula, and "the warble"!). Here is an opportunity to appropriate the classic principle of *abusus non tollit usus*: abuses do not nullify uses. We must not dismiss the whole of this great treasure based upon its inclusion of superstitious verse. To do so would rob us of the great many God-honoring prayers in the *Carmina* that can be helpful to us today.

To those prayers we now turn.

Morning Prayers

I am convicted by the *Carmina's* collection of morning prayers, for they reveal how hastily I rush into the business of each day. I squelch my chirping alarm and my mind automatically moves into get-ready mode. Rarely do I stop to consider, as these Highland pray-ers did, that God has sustained each and every one of my breaths throughout the night.

> *Thanks to Thee ever, O gentle Christ,*
> *That Thou hast raised me freely from the black*

And from the darkness of last night
To the kindly light of this day. [16]

If we are truly in search of a renewed and vigorous life with God, we might begin by giving greater consideration to the miracle of awakening each morning. The rhythm of sleeping and waking is, in itself, an analogy of our own death and resurrection; yet our waking moments pass without considering it and giving thanks.

The *Carmina Gadelica* shows that upon waking, a simple prayer in the threefold pattern would be prayed with each splash of water on the face:

The palmful of the God of Life,
The palmful of the Christ of Love,
The Palmful of the Spirit of Peace,
Triune
Of Grace. [17]

My own morning routine usually takes me in my groggy, pajama-ed state to the kitchen for a stop at the tea-station, then on to the study where I do my best to listen to God for awhile. These can be sweet times, for the Lord's mercies truly are new with each morning. But there are also some sleepy times, and some frustrating times, and times that I oversleep and don't make it at all. I am heartened to read the Celtic "Prayer at Rising," which encourages me to be more thoughtful as I commit a given day to God:

Bless to me, O God,
Each thing mine eye sees;
Bless to me, O God,
Each sound mine ear hears;
Bless to me, O God,
Each odour that goes to my nostrils;
Bless to me, O God,
Each taste that goes to my lips;
Each note that goes to my song,
Each ray that guides my way,

Each thing that I pursue,
Each lure that tempts my will,
The zeal that seeks my living soul,
The Three that seek my heart,
The zeal that seeks my living soul,
The Three that seek my heart.[18]

One of my favorite Highland prayers is found in the "Cattle-Stock" section of the *Gadelica:*

Bless, O God, my little cow,
Bless, O God, my desire;
Bless Thou my partnership
And the milking of my hands, O God.[19]

This prayer continues, asking God to bless "each drop that goes into my pitcher." On one hand, it reminds me of the prayers that we learn as children, blessing everyone and everything one can think of. On the other, I see the pure intention to honor God with even the earthiest of tasks, and a conviction that the smallest drop of milk has the potential to reflect the glory of God. Such a prayer acknowledges that all creatures and tasks fall under the loving purview of God, and that we not only depend upon him to bless our efforts, but we accept our role as co-laborers, as *partners* with God in the work that he is doing in the world—even if it is only the work of providing nourishment through the milk of a cow. What a wonderful connection-point is found here between the one who is milking and the One who made the cow! They are working together in a three-way act that is now made holy by this simple, sanctifying prayer.

There were also prayers for weaving:

Bless, O Chief of generous chiefs,
My loom and everything anear me,
Bless me in every action,
Make Thou me safe while I live. . . .
Every web, black, white, and fair,
Roan, dun, checked, and red,

Give Thy blessing everywhere,
On every shuttle passing under the thread.[20]

And prayers for sheep-herding:

May the Spirit of peace preserve the flocks,
May the Son of Mary Virgin preserve the flocks,
May the God of glory preserve the flocks,
May the Three preserve the flocks,
From wounding and from death-loss,
From wounding and from death-loss.[21]

As we begin working on our computers, do we intentionally consecrate the work of our hands for the honor and glory of God? Or the cell phones we use, by which we will connect with other human beings and have the chance to bless them rather than curse? Perhaps many of us would say with confidence that we easily and naturally commit our overt acts of ministry to God: "Bless this mission team," or "Bless this worship service," or "Bless these funds that we give for Your work." What does not come so naturally is to commit to God the very ordinary, mundane tasks and tools of our day, even though we know, of course, that *all* things can be used by God and for God. We are simply not in the habit, the spiritual discipline, of consecrating all aspects of our days to God, moment by moment.

What a simple thing "praying without ceasing" would be if we would determine to place all things, from the mean to the celebrated, into God's hands. When we live in ongoing awareness of the reality of the living God—yes, the one who is right beside me even now as I type these words—we are praying without ceasing. When I get in my car tomorrow morning to drive to the courthouse to contest my speeding ticket, I will acknowledge that Jesus is in the car with me (and will be with me when I "make my case" no matter what the outcome). Even that can be prayer.

My "soul friend" Sally has instinctively applied a pattern of praying to her daily work that helps her regularly invite God into her life at every turn. Sally is a dental professional in downtown Seattle, working in a high-rise office building in the midst of exquisite shopping malls, high-powered businesses, and the ubiquitous Starbucks shops. For many years she has expertly wed her dental practice with prayer by "praying on teeth," as she says. Apparently in the world of dentistry each human tooth is given a number, and Sally has matched each tooth and its number to specific family members, friends, and particular needs. So, while Sally cleans a patient's teeth, she will pray for those particular names and needs depending on what tooth she happens to be cleaning. She smiles when she assures me that she's assigned a tooth to me that, for most patients, generally needs a lot of attention—which translates into more time spent praying for me! This method of praying intrigues me, because it is so extraordinary in its ordinariness. Sally uses what she has, which happens to be a whole lot of teeth every day. Instead of complaining about the impossibility of "praying without ceasing," of doing all things in the presence of God, Sally has figured out a natural way to be spiritually engaged. She hasn't sought a new technique; she simply incorporates prayer into her daily routine. It is in this routine that Sally has found what the early Christian Celts discovered long ago: God is ready to sanctify our most basic actions in ways that increase our awareness of and dependence on him.

A final example from the *Carmina Gadelica* reveals a Highland woman praying as she "smoors" or banks down the peat fire for the night. Again, she does so in the name of the Trinity:

The sacred Three
To save,
To shield,
To surround
The hearth,
The house,
The household,
This eve,
This night,
Oh! This eve,
This night,

And every night,
Each single night.
Amen.[22]

When I read these prayers they create for me an image—not of a superstitious woman who feels the need to cast a spell around her home to ward off evil spirits—but of a lover of a living, present God who is accessible enough to come close and surround her home with the loving protection of a Heavenly Father, a Divine Son, and a Holy Spirit. This is the same God I worship, but in a modern time and in a home with an automatic heat source that only needs its thermostat adjusted. Yet this Triune God offers the same presence to me, and in a mysterious way even links me with this believing Highland woman of old. She teaches me that our prayers are not distinguished by eloquence or volume but by our desire for God, and that "the Sacred Three" would, like intricate Celtic knotwork, seep into each crevice of our lives in an endless, interactive pattern.

Praying the Psalms

Another way monastic communities tried to pray at all times was by gathering at five different times each day to corporately pray the Psalms. Ian Bradley helps us understand this pattern:

> Five times during the day, at the hours of prime, terce, sext, nones and vespers, and three times during the hours of darkness, at nightfall, at midnight and very early in the morning toward daybreak, the monks gathered, summoned by a bell. By far the greatest part of each office consisted of chanting the Psalms in Latin. Irish monks seem to have worked their way through the entire cycle of 150 psalms more quickly than those in Continental orders. They sang more of them at each service and they also met together more often to worship during the night. . . . There are echoes of this practice in the depiction of Columba in the twelfth-century Irish Life rattling through all 150 psalms (the "three fifties") before sunrise every

morning as he lay on the beach on Iona after sleeping for just a few hours. . . .[23]

The author of Psalm 119 reveals that he prayed "seven times a day" (Ps. 119:164), and Daniel's faithfulness is celebrated, for the "three times a day he got down on his knees and prayed, giving thanks to his God" (Dan. 6:10). Praying at regular, fixed times is a discipline that was in place in biblical times, and one that the Celtic and European monastics believed to be worthy of emulation.

Blessing

Finally, we must say a word about the Celtic inclination to bless. Here is another way that our modern culture has missed out on the great Christian heritage of our ancestors in the British Isles. For when most of us think of "blessing" and "Irish" in the same context, we're limited to our feeble attempt to recite "May the Road Rise Up to Meet Ye." This is but a cursory glimpse into the great treasure of the Celtic tradition of blessing which is, as Bradley states, "one of the most marked characteristics of the continuing legacy of a distinctive Celtic Christianity in the religious life and literature of Ireland, Wales and the Scottish Highlands and islands over the last thirteen hundred years or so."[24]

In pre-Christian days, the Celts had "a very strong sense of the almost physical power of the spoken word both to heal and to harm."[25] Pagan bards were among the most revered in the tribe, memorizing poetry and stories to preserve their traditions. In fact, it was believed that "the spoken word cannot be frozen in written form or it will lose its life."[26] Bards were present in war to verbally provoke the enemy, as well as at the birth of babies, greeting the child with songs and poems.[27]

It is in the act of blessing, then, that we see yet another example of the redemptive power of God. Pagan practices are changed for holy purposes, incorporating an eloquent art form that hearkens back to the earliest Hebrew Scriptures. These new Christians no longer called upon pagan deities, but instead invoked the blessing of Father, Son, and Holy Spirit.

May the King shield you in the valleys,
May Christ aid you on the mountains,
May Spirit bathe you on the slopes,
In hollow, on hill, on plain,
Mountain, valley and plain.[28]

"In the end, all blessing simply means being close to God, declaring the proximity and reciprocity of all goodness in the divine bounty," writes Robert Woods.[29] This is not unfamiliar to us, because we've read the benedictions that Paul pronounced upon his friends:

"The grace of the Lord Jesus Christ be with your spirit." (Phil 4:23)
"The grace of our Lord Jesus Christ be with you." (I Thess 5:23)
"The grace of our Lord Jesus Christ be with you all" (II Thess 3:18)
"The Lord be with your spirit. Grace be with you." (II Tim. 4:22)
"The grace of the Lord Jesus Christ be with your spirit." (Phile.1:23)

Paul's repeated blessing of grace clearly meets Robert Woods' criteria for a "blessing" given above, for grace is among the greatest examples of the goodness of God. In the same way we hear the Pauline ring echoing in this Gaelic blessing:

The keeping of God and the Lord on you,
The keeping of Christ always on you,
. . . the peace-giving Spirit, everlasting, be yours,
The peace-giving Spirit, everlasting, be yours.[30]

Like Paul, these descendants of the earliest Christians in the British Isles were conveying to the recipient "in an almost physical sense a portion of God's goodness and grace."[31] However, in the Celtic tradition blessings could be pronounced by any Christian, not just by monks or other clergy. "They were emphatically not confined to liturgical use but had a prominent place in the everyday lives and conversation of laity and clergy alike, both inside and beyond the monastic *vallum* (boundary)."[32]

Many years ago when our youngest daughter, Langley, was just an infant, we had a very personal experience of what it means to be blessed by another believer. We had experienced sacramental blessing when we formally dedicated her to the Lord in a church ceremony, as well as years later at her baptism. But this particular time blessing came to us, and to her, in a delightfully surprising way.

For much of my adult life I have been significantly influenced by the writing and teaching ministry of Richard Foster. I first read his book *Celebration of Discipline* (selected by *Christianity Today* as one of the top ten religious books of the twentieth century) as a college student, my first edition copy still bearing my maiden name. His book *Prayer: Finding the Heart's True Home* is a book that I return to again and again, and have passed on to a number of friends and students. And his very helpful work on the six traditions of the Church, *Streams of Living Water*, serves as a text for the course I teach at John Brown University.

Sometime before Langley was born, I learned that Dr. Foster would be coming to our area to lead a workshop. I immediately carved the date onto my calendar. I knew that my new baby would be only eight weeks old at the time of the workshop, yet I was determined to attend.

In the end, it wasn't so easy, as Langley was a bit of a fusser as an infant. Nevertheless, kind members of the hosting church recognized my ordeal with her that day and set me up in the "crying room" with an earpiece so I could still hear Dr. Foster speak. After the service the first night, I marched right up to the stage, Langley in tow, to thank him in person for the many ways his ministry had helped my journey of faith.

Dr. Foster was exceedingly gracious, of course, but in the middle of our conversation, I noticed his attention became diverted. He fixed his eyes on Langley. He kindly asked about her—her name, how old she was—smiling with amusement that I would bring such a young one to his workshop. Then came the surprise. "Will Langley be joining us tomorrow?" he asked. I assured him she was. "I wonder if you'd bring her up front during our worship time so we could all bless her?"

The next day I dressed her in her fluffy white "Daddy loves me" sleeper, smiling as I thought about the double meaning: loved by Cary, loved by God. Later that morning, during the service, Dr. Foster did indeed call us up to the stage and introduced Langley as the "youngest attender" at the workshop. He took her in his arms and prayed a beautiful blessing over her. And then he whispered something in her ear, which remains a three-way secret between Dr. Foster, Langley, and God.

Was it a special thrill that one of my "virtual mentors" chose to bless my child? Certainly. But the deepest joy came from the act of blessing itself, speaking those powerful words and believing that by God's grace they make a difference.

How would an unbelieving world respond if the Body of Christ became known more for our words of blessing than our words of critique? I am in no way suggesting that all behaviors and choices should be blessed by the church. What I am considering is how many opportunities we miss to literally bless others—with words—and how the repossession of this ancient art could play a role in channeling the love and power of God to the world. *But they're just words*, someone might argue. And yet it was "just words" that spoke the world into being and "just words" that became incarnate as the Son of God.

Blessings need not be eloquent or poetic. A modern, to-the-point blessing I love is, "Go with God!" It seems to say it all when a departure of importance is at hand—leaving for kindergarten/college, a critical meeting, or an event requiring extra courage. I also love the way liturgical churches "pass the peace" to each other during the usual "greet your neighbor" time in the worship service. To think of the power in those simple words: "The peace of Christ to you." Isn't Christ's peace one of the most powerful, life-changing, place-of-resurrection things we could give to one another?

Peace between neighbors
Peace between kindred,
Peace between lovers,
In love of the King of life.

Peace between person and person,
Peace between wife and husband,
Peace between woman and children,

The peace of Christ above all peace.

Bless, O Christ, my face,
Let my face bless every thing;
Bless, O Christ, mine eye,
Let mine eye bless all it sees.[33]

The Celts—the earliest Christians in Ireland and Scotland, and their Highland descendants centuries later—knew the power of the word in prayer and in blessing. And because they did it so easily, throughout the dailiness of their lives, they have demonstrated to us that "praying without ceasing" can be as easy as breathing out and in.

May we, too, become vessels of God through the spoken word.

Celtic Blessing

Be the eye of God dwelling with you,
The food of Christ in guidance with you,
The shower of the Spirit pouring on you,
Richly and generously.
God's peace be to you,
Jesus' peace be to you,
Spirit's peace be to you
And to your children,
Oh to you and to your children,
Each day and night
Of your portion in the world.[34]

Meditation: Colossians 3:15-17

Let the peace of Christ rule in your hearts, since as members of one body you were called to peace. And be thankful. Let the word of Christ dwell in you richly as you teach and admonish one another with all wisdom, and as you sing psalms, hymns and spiritual songs with gratitude in your hearts to

God. And whatever you do, whether in word or deed, do it all in the name of the Lord Jesus, giving thanks to God the Father through him.

Reflection Questions

1. Who taught you to pray? What was the first prayer you ever learned to pray? How has your praying changed since then?

2. What are the "ordinary" moments of a typical day that could be sanctified by your prayers? Think of one piece of equipment you use every day (just one, to begin): a car, a cell phone, a computer, a bicycle, a checkbook. Make its use an occasion for prayer.

3. Consider using your journal to write out simple, ordinary prayers and blessings. Let it be a spiritual discipline to train you for "the real thing".

FOUR

PILGRIMAGE

From Exile to the Promised Land

Iona Journal

Cary and I have just returned from an afternoon hike to St. Columba's Bay. I've done this hike on my own before, so I was eager to introduce Cary to the south end of the island. We had the amazing gift of another beautiful day; the temperature was brisk and perfect for walking. Before heading out, we stopped at the tiny grocery store to purchase a bottle of water and a couple of snacks.

We followed the path southward along the shoreline, Iona's stunning turquoise water to our left, cottages and farms to our right. Eventually it was time to turn inland and then south again toward the bay. The two of us marveled at the cottages that dotted the shoreline and the landscape, bearing Gaelic names like "Tigh na Mara," "Dun Craig," and "The Durran." *Who lives here? What do they do?* And I can't help chuckling at the lambs and their mothers. It always sounds to me as if the lambs are calling out "Mom? Maaahm?" The mama sheep, recognizing her baby's voice, will respond vocally from the other side of the pasture. Then the funny little lamb will scamper across to where Mom is. I guess I am a city girl, because this is completely amusing to me.

Finally, the bay came into view. Columba's Bay is known geologically for its vast amounts of sea-worn rocks all along its shore. Centuries of pounding waves have worn the rocks so smooth that when the water draws back away from the beach, the rocks roll back with it, making an enchanting tinkling sound as they do. Not only are the rocks plentiful, they are also beautiful. So many different colors and striations to be found—olive green, rust red, brilliant white, sparkling pink granite and glowing agate. And if one is fortunate, you will find a piece of Iona marble, which was once mined from the marble quarry on the southeast end of the island and can now be seen in the form of the great green-white altar at the front of the Iona Abbey sanctuary.

Cary and I found a boulder to perch on and began eating our snacks when a group of hikers descended to the beach alongside us. We quickly discerned that this was a "pilgrimage" group from the Abbey. Once a week or so the Iona Community leads a pilgrimage around the island, visiting the various sites of religious significance and praying as they go. They and we were there at the bay to enjoy its beauty, but also to visit the place where Columba, the missionary/monk from Ireland, arrived in his small boat with his friends to begin a new missional community.

We heard the pilgrimage guide point out the high rocky hill where Columba climbed to confirm that he could no longer see his beloved Ireland. Once he did, his band of monks knew this would be the location for their community. The leader then went on to reflect on what it meant to leave an old life behind and move forward to a new life with God. He paralleled this to Christ's crucifixion and resurrection, and asked his group of pilgrims what they needed to let die in order that they might rise again to new life. He then instructed them each to pick up two of the smooth stones on the beach. They were to throw one stone in the ocean, representing what they would like to leave behind; the second stone they were to keep, representing the new thing they would like to take with them to wherever their homes might be.

Cary asked me what I wanted to leave behind. I felt so full of blessing being there on Iona (represented by my ziplock bag of colorful stones I'd collected at the bay), I wasn't sure I had anything to leave behind. It took less than two minutes of thought to recognize that of course there was something in my life that God was asking me to leave behind, to put to death so that he could redeem and resurrect something new.

I found a big smooth rock the size of a large baking potato, and I hurled it into the sea where it landed with a great *ka-chunk*....

[handwritten margin note: what needs to die?]

"Your life is a journey you must travel
with a deep consciousness of God."
1 Peter 1:17 (The Message)

When friends return from vacation, we naturally ask them, "How was your vacation?" "What did you do?" "What did you see?" When was the last time I intentionally asked, "What did it *mean*?"

Traveling and tourism is a massive industry today. Many of us, when asked the question, "If you could do anything, what would it be?" would say that we'd love to travel to some far-off or exotic destination. Our Celtic ancestors in faith shared our wanderlust. Their purpose in journeying, however, was fairly different from that of most modern travelers, for they did not leave their homes for pleasure or business or to satisfy curiosity. For the early Christian Celts, journeying was an exercise undertaken for the love of God.

A curious Latin name is given to this practice: *peregrinatio*, which when translated can mean either "pilgrimage" or "voluntary abandonment of home and kin for ascetic purposes."[1] This magnetic pull towards journeying is a distinguishing mark of early Celtic Christianity. Unlike the conventional understanding of pilgrimage in which people journey to shrines to venerate the relics of saints, the Celts traveled without a distinct destiny in mind. They learned that it is not so much the final destination that brings us to greater Christlikeness, but the *process* of journeying itself.

Here we see the ultimate purpose of *peregrinatio*: seeking to identify with Christ in his death. "This was seen as a way of following Christ in his 'self-emptying.' Just as Christ let go of his divinity to fully embrace humanity, so the monk would let go of his beloved land to follow Christ."[2] The *peregrini* went on pilgrimage to "seek the place of their resurrection," setting out for an unknown location in hopes that God would meet them face to face and perhaps even usher them into eternity,[3] which was, they believed, the greatest journey of all.

What would it have been like to set out on pilgrimage without any knowledge of one's final destination? What was such a journey like at that time in history? It was certainly much more adventurous and risky than the kind of traveling we generally embark upon. Living in the British Isles necessitated a water journey if one were to truly empty oneself and leave one's homeland. The vessel of choice was the *curach*, a vessel made from oxhide stretched over a wooden frame, usually large enough to carry fourteen passengers and their supplies.[4] These simple craft were seaworthy enough; it was the threat of Viking marauders or stormy seas that made the journey so treacherous. In Lawhead's novel *Byzantium* we read a fictional account of Irish *peregrini* braving the tempest as it threatened to tear their *curach* apart:

> Through the long darkness we prayed and comforted one another as best we could. The night wore on and on, endless, gradually passing to day once more with little alteration in the light. Day or night, the darkness remained heavy as the waves towered over us on every side. . . . We huddled in the bottom of the boat, clinging each to the other and all to the grain sacks. Bishop Cadoc, cold to the bone, shivering and shuddering, offered a continual litany of psalms and prayers of deliverance. The men of Eire [Ireland] are a seagoing tribe and we have many invocations of an oceanic nature. The good bishop knew them all and spoke them twice, and then said as many more that I had never heard before. . . .
>
> All through the tempest-tortured night we shivered and prayed, the scream of wind and thunder of water loud in our ears. Hard pressed though we were, we kept courage keen with faith in God and hope of deliverance.
>
> Even when the rudder pin gave way, we did not despair. Mael and Fintan hauled the broken rudder aboard and lashed

it securely to the side of the boat. "We are at the mercy of the wind now," Mael informed us.

"Let Him who fixed the pole star guide us," Cadoc replied. "Lord, we are in your hand. Send us where you will."[5]

Some of the hagiographic tales of these seafaring voyagers are fantastic indeed, the stories of St. Brendan the Navigator being among the most famous. Brendan, who lived in the sixth century in southwestern Ireland, was the epitome of the *peregrini*. As a monk and abbot, his reputation as a pilgrim grew through his visits to Columba on Iona, to Wales and to Brittany. His greatest voyage was one of voluntary exile, setting out to "follow God without a plan, not on the land, but in a frail boat. . . . Brendan and twelve of his companions set sail from the Dingle Peninsula, seeking God's 'Island of Promise' at some vague location in the Atlantic Ocean, trusting totally in the mercy of God to lead them to their destination."[6] Lest we be tempted to entertain idealistic notions about Brendan's reckless abandon, pilgrimage expert Cintra Pemberton brings a corrective word:

> Romantic as such total (irrational?) dependence on God may seem, and as often as such a viewpoint is presented in some books about Celtic spirituality, the reality is not quite that simple. The Celtic seafarers, Brendan included, were extremely experienced at reading the sky, the wind, sea currents, and weather patterns. When setting sail out into the unknown, the Celtic gyrovague[7] sailors had great trust in God, to be sure, but they also had a far greater knowledge of the sea than is usually acknowledged. All these wanderers for God simply took off, on land or on sea, following some indescribable internal pull to wherever, but knowing clearly that the inner pull came from God and was to be followed, no matter where it might lead.[8]

Journeying and Praying

Although time and civilization continued to advance, journeying continued as a distinctive of the Celtic culture in Ireland, Scotland, England,
Wales, and the Isle of Man. In the *Carmina Gadelica* we see the importance of spoken blessings and prayers over the *peregrini* before setting
out on their journeys. The following "journey prayer" illustrates the Celtic
devotion to the Trinity while extending a heartfelt blessing to the one
who is traveling:

> *God be with thee in every pass,*
> *Jesus be with thee on every hill,*
> *Spirit be with thee on every stream,*
>> *Headland and ridge and lawn;*
> *Each sea and land, each moor and meadow,*
> *Each lying down, each rising up,*
> *In the trough of the waves, on the crest of the billows,*
>> *Each step of the journey thou goest.*[9]

A number of other entries in Carmichael's collection remind us of the
strong Celtic perception of the presence of God surrounding them at all
times, confirmed and affirmed by the prayer attributed to St. Patrick which
calls upon Christ to be beside, before, behind, beneath, and below. The
concept of "compassing," of dwelling in a circle of God's protection, was
surely comforting as one embarked upon an uncertain journey.

> *The compassing of God be on thee,*
> *The compassing of the God of life.*

> *The compassing of Christ be on thee,*
> *The compassing of the Christ of love.*

> *The compassing of Spirit be on thee,*
> *The compassing of the Spirit of Grace.*

> *The compassing of the Three be on thee,*
> *The compassing of the Three preserve thee,*
> *The compassing of the Three preserve thee.*[10]

How much more meaningful our own journeys would be if someone gave us such a blessing as we go! Consider another prayer from the *Carmina Gadelica*, asking for the protective, surrounding presence of God, simple in structure, yet so beautifully articulated:

The compassing of God and His right hand
Be upon my form and upon my frame;
The compassing of the High King and the grace of the Trinity
 Be upon me abiding ever eternally,
 Be upon me abiding ever eternally.

May the compassing of the Three shield me in my means,
The compassing of the Three shield me this day,
The compassing of the Three shield me this night
 From hate, from harm, from act, from ill,
 From hate, from harm, from act, from ill.[11]

These prayers and blessings not only illustrate the Celtic dependence on God for their journeying, but, as we discussed earlier, they teach us a great deal about prayer itself. For example, Carmichael's collection reveals a great beauty and artistry in the crafting of these prayers, helping us see once again that the Celtic faith was truly an earthy existence and not without pain and suffering. *Peregrinatio*, like the journeying of Christ himself, often tested the journeyer to the point of anguish.

Relieve Thou, O God, each one
In suffering on land or sea,
In grief or wounded or weeping,
And lead them to the house of Thy peace
 This night.

I am weary, weak and cold,
I am weary of traveling land and sea,
I am weary of traversing moorland and billow,
Grant me peace in the nearness of Thy repose
 This night.[12]

At the same time, *peregrini* found great joy in the journey. They celebrated the calling of God on their lives, singing, laughing, and expressing the joy that comes in walking with Christ himself:

My walk this day with God,
My walk this day with Christ,
My walk this day with Spirit.
The threefold all-kindly:
Ho! Ho! Ho! The Threefold all-kindly.

My shielding this day from ill,
My shielding this night from harm,
Ho! Ho! Both my soul and my body,
Be by Father, by Son, by Holy Spirit:
By Father, by Son, by Holy Spirit.

Be the Father shielding me,
Be the Son shielding me,
Be the Spirit shielding me,
As Three and as One:
Ho! Ho! Ho! As Three and as One.[13]

Finally, in a poem credited to the great *peregrini*, Columba, we hear the prayer of one who is not content to ask only for protection for himself; the prayer asks for the circle of God's presence to be extended outwards to everyone he encounters:

The path I walk, Christ walks it. May the land in
    Which I am be without sorrow.
May the Trinity protect me wherever I stay, Father,
    Son, and Holy Spirit.
Bright angels walk with me—dear presence—in every
    Dealing.
In every dealing I pray them that no one's poison
    May reach me.
The ninefold people of heaven of holy cloud, the

Tenth force of the stone earth.
Favorable company, they come with me, so that the
Lord may not be angry with me.
May I arrive at every place, may I return home; may
The way in which I spend be a way without loss.
May every path before me be smooth, man, woman
And child welcome me.
A truly good journey! Well does the fair Lord show
us a course, a path.[14]

Ancient Journeys

Finding models of this journeying tradition in the pages of Scripture is not difficult. As Yahweh called to Abram, asking him to leave his country, people, and father's household, it came with a great promise of transformation: from one man into countless people, from obscurity to great honor and blessing, from isolation to covenant with God himself. Such a transformation required a name change, and Abram became Abraham to signify the event (Gen 17:5). Abraham embodied the very character of *peregrinatio* as he left for a foreign land. He went not out of curiosity or wanderlust, but in obedience to the call of God, asking him to sacrifice what is familiar.

Moses serves as a model as well, but for a different reason. His flight from Pharaoh in Egypt to Midian contains more elements of exile and penance, which are also characteristics of some of the Celtic *peregrinatio*. The years Moses spent in the desert became his years of training, preparing him for the role he was to play in Hebrew history.

Other models for this more ascetic approach to journeying were the desert fathers and mothers, devout believers who retreated into the deserts of Egypt for the purpose of communing with God. Geoffrey Moorehouse elaborates:

> They were not fleeing from something they disliked or mistrusted or were polluted or persecuted by, though some of them

had been persecuted, like all believers at that time. They were not taking refuge in the desert as someone without faith might see it, out of fear of the alternative. They desired more than anything else to see God, to behold Christ's face, to know Him as He was, now and forever, awaiting them in heaven above. They were impatient for death, though this last and greatest blessing could only be granted them in God's good time and not a moment of their own choosing, which would have been blasphemy. There was nothing else that mattered to them other than the desire for heavenly union, and they wished to prepare for it, to purify themselves and thus be worthy, to make it more certainly theirs, without the slightest distraction. That was all they were fleeing from: the distractions of the villages and towns that would hold them back from more than the possibility of God's grace. They did want much more than the possibility.[15]

The Celtic *peregrini* sometimes embarked on their journeys with the purpose of being purified and disciplined for greater works of service, thus giving them their reputation as "athletes of God." Hagiographers of the Celtic saints have given us many accounts of these ascetic practices, exercises of "strict self-denial with the spiritual goal of cleansing oneself of sin and focusing the mind on God alone."[16] Tradition tells us, for example, that Columba's bed was bare rock, his pillow a stone. (Carved into this stone is the Celtic cross; it can be seen in the museum adjacent to Iona Abbey.) Other Celtic saints, like Kevin of Glendalough, were said to pray for long hours with arms extended in the form of a cross while standing in the frigid waters of a mountain stream. They took on back-breaking manual labor, wore hair shirts or chains for penance, and isolated themselves for long periods of time. These were all common ascetic practices.[17]

The monks of Skellig Michael, the rugged island monastery off the Dingle Coast of Ireland, serve as another vivid example of sacrificial *peregrinatio*, living as they did on the very margins of civilization; cut off from the larger community, accessible only by those who would bravely traverse unpredictable seas to reach their harsh rocky settlement. Skellig

Michael's remains tell us much about the austere life of the small band of monks, its stone beehive huts still surprisingly intact after more than a thousand years. Modern pilgrims can still visit the site when the weather cooperates—if one doesn't lose the nerve required to climb the steep steps up to the top of the sharply rising cliffs.

Such examples may rub against our modern sensibilities, not only because they just sound bizarre (Were they taking the Apostle Paul literally when he spoke of beating his body and making it his slave? [1 Cor. 9:27]), but also because we so firmly believe that salvation comes by faith alone. Such extreme practices would seem to indicate an improper understanding of our role in working out our own salvation (Phil. 2:12).

Our concern here is certainly justified. The Celtic saint Columbanus (not to be confused with Columba of Iona) emphatically proclaimed that "mere mortification of the flesh is useless. It is only a tool toward the real goal of stripping one's self of all desires and possessions that can bind one to the present world."[18] We can see why God called Abram away from "home and hearth" and why Moses had to be removed from what was familiar to him. The love of what is dear and familiar to us can be a great obstacle in our relationship with a God who asks for all and nothing less.

Here we can again apply the "abuses do not nullify uses" principle. If we truly need to find the place of our resurrection, to discover our "deepest and truest self in Christ,"[19] we'd best be willing to learn from and adapt the *best* of what our Christian forebears practiced.

Guests of the World

A final motivation toward *peregrinatio*—and this is perhaps the one we can be most grateful for—was the Celtic call to mission and evangelism. The earliest Celts in Ireland were fiercely attached to their land, a land completely and astonishingly preserved from Roman occupation. However, with the Gospel came a missional drive, and many became *peregrini* for the sake of expanding the kingdom of God. This description certainly fits Patrick, who, as one of the first great *peregrini*, willingly responded to the call of God and left all he loved to take the gospel to those in Ireland who had once enslaved him. Likewise, the story of Columba is distinguished by self-emptying, exile, and a call to expand the kingdom of God, which resulted in the founding of Iona in the sixth century.

The list goes on, including Aidan, "who went from Iona in the seventh century to Lindisfarne, and whose monks converted Northumbria to Christianity; and St. Columbanus, abbot of Bangor (now Northern Ireland), who set out for France, and then crossed the Alps into Italy, and who at Bobbio made a foundation which was to surpass all other in fame and achievement."[20] Their journeys, as Thomas Cahill boldly asserts, "saved civilization,"[21] for they put into motion the re-evangelization of the British Isles and the preservation of literacy throughout Medieval Europe.

Peregrinatio Today

It has been said that the longest journey is the journey inward.[22] *Peregrinatio* helps us convert our modern understanding of tourism (which in itself is, for the most part, morally neutral) and enhance it, making it an experience of eternal value. The final goal of the pilgrimage or journey becomes, ultimately, spiritual transformation into the image of Jesus himself; or as Cintra Pemberton explains, "interior growth resulting from an exterior journey."[23]

I love the concept of pilgrimage because it gives me a greater sense of purpose in my various travels hither and yon. Whether it is a trip out of the country or a small journey within a day's drive, the Celtic *peregrini* have modeled a particular posture that is easily adapted, no matter what my final destination might be. That posture, that attitude, encourages me to be undertaking this journey simply out of love for God. It creates in me a holy expectation: that even in the most ordinary parts of getting from here to there (perhaps especially the ordinary), God will make his presence known to me. Through that experience, I may well find a "place of resurrection" where new life is coaxed up from the grave of spiritual complacency.

Sometimes it comes with a dose of humor. One evening on Iona, Cary and I left our seaside hotel to walk to the Abbey for services. Just a few paces from the hotel doorway is a path lined with fuchsia hedges, a shortcut to the main road that leads to the Abbey. We walked those few paces, took the sharp left to turn onto the path, and found ourselves standing face to face with a large mama sheep and her two lambs! The three of them took up the entire width of the path, and as they resolutely stood there it became clear there would be no getting around them. Cary and I just laughed as we looked at the expression on that mama sheep's face, a look that said, "So then, who's going to budge, you or me?" We submissively moved to either side of the path, gladly deferring to her and encouraged her to walk on through. She proudly pranced by, the two lambies following obediently, while we laughed at the sight of it.

Encounters like this are delightful gifts, yet I do not take them lightly. I learned from poet Luci Shaw that the most ordinary moments in life can be "numinous"—charged with meaning beyond themselves, making the ordinary extra-ordinary. At that moment of "the sheep encounter" on Iona, I thanked God for his whimsical artistry in designing the creatures of this world, and for our surprising rendezvous with three of them.

Another way we gain a sense of purpose on our journeys is through engaging in conversations with folks who are also journeying, and with those who live and work in the places we visit. I must confess that when it comes to striking up conversations with people I don't know, I am a squeamish introvert. For whatever reason—blame it on my Myers-Briggs type—I generally find it very awkward to chat with strangers or new acquaintances. To tell the truth, one of the least favorite moments in my whole week is when we are asked to smile and greet one another at church. I dutifully cooperate, but in the end I usually wimp out, seeking refuge with someone I already know.

Now here's the irony. When I've had the privilege of going to Iona on pilgrimage, one of my favorite parts of it is smiling and greeting other pilgrims at the Abbey services. Go figure! Here's the reason: when you're on Iona and worshiping in the Abbey, chances are that the folks you're worshiping with have a particular reason for being there. And I find myself desperate to find out what it is. I have met many lovely and fascinating fellow-pilgrims from all over the world: a college student from Africa, an Iona community worker from Canada, a young female theology student from Germany. As we chat we become aware of how different we are from each other, just by virtue of our cultures. Yet the commonality of seeking and worshiping God overrides the superficial differences, uniting us for that brief moment in time in a way that nourishes my soul.

Conversing with the local folk is equally enriching, for it not only gives us a deeper understanding of the particular place we are visiting, it expands our appreciation for the great creative scope of God's image as presented in every human face. One of my fondest memories of visiting Ireland is of having a cup of tea in an Irish home. Our Irish professors that year were Liz and Paddy Roche, dear folk who loved the Lord, held positions of great influence in their communities (Liz was a member of their City Council; Paddy a member of the Northen Ireland Parliament), and were hospitable in the extreme. This particular afternoon I felt especially blessed because it was just my friend Becci and I who were invited for tea at the Roche home. There in their cozy sitting room were five very different women: "Gran" in her easy chair, her crocheted throw across her lap; Helen, the Roche's beautiful young daughter with a lilting accent, attending to our needs; Liz, the consummate hostess, bringing out not just one elaborate dessert for us, but three or four; Becci, my American co-leader and friend; and myself, holding my "wee cuppa" and marveling at this gift of being able to experience Irish life first-hand. The differences present among us melted away as we shared our lives over a simple cup of tea. Dear Liz has since gone to heaven. I look forward to sharing another cup of tea with her one day.

Our journeying also brings us face to face with profound truth. Leading university students on study trips to Ireland has expanded my own world, for as leaders my husband and I are responsible not only for teaching these students as we travel around the island, but also for the multiple dimensions of their well-being. It is an incredibly stretching experience, personally and spiritually.

The really significant "aha" moments consistently happen for all of us when we visit the inner city of Belfast. There the Shankill Road marks a neighborhood that for decades has been a centerpiece for violent acts of hatred between the Protestants and Catholics who make Belfast their home. These designations are given not primarily because of religion but because of politics, and their dissension has resulted in the violent deaths of many men, women and children over the years. Thus "The Troubles"— the name given to decades of terrorism—have marked this city forever. Thankfully, there has been a season of relatively undisturbed peace between the groups in recent years.

One year on the Irish studies trip, my husband made arrangements for our students to meet with a gentleman who had formerly been an active member of one of the most violent paramilitary groups in Belfast. "Ace" had served time in prison for murder and had since then given his life to Christ; now Ace was actively involved in a reconciliation ministry among Protestants and Catholics. Ace gave us a personal tour of the Shankill neighborhood, pointing out places where bombs had gone off or where people had been gunned down. He showed us row upon row of murals painted on the sides of neighborhood buildings; it was propaganda created to memorialize fallen soldiers in the paramilitary and to graphically remind anyone who trespassed that they were crossing over into "enemy" territory.

These kinds of experiences that confront us on our journey cry out for our attention, offering us new and transforming insights if we have the courage to be open to the transforming process. We can ask, *What does such an experience mean? How am I different because of it? What does it teach me about the world? What does God think of all of this?*

My friend and colleague Shirley Thomas uses a term that we've adopted in our study abroad programs, and it's one that would be useful for each of us who long to take the pilgrimage of our lives seriously. The term, "place as text," is a way of saying that the places we visit serve as textbooks to us if we will but "read" them. Textbooks are written to impart knowledge; likewise, the world was created to impart wisdom

Diff
of
tourist
+
pilgrim

(Psalm 104:24). Perhaps that is another way of understanding the differ-ence between the attitude of a tourist and the attitude of a pilgrim. On one journey we set out to gain knowledge; on another we set out to gain wisdom.

Conclusion

To go on pilgrimage in the late twentieth century is un-questionably, at one level, to be a tourist (i.e., one who travels around), but at a much deeper and more life-changing level, it is to travel in such a way that our restlessness (or perhaps we might call it our wanderlust) is always searching for God, even as God is searching for us. On our pilgrimage, we are all soulfarers together. Each of us makes the conscious choice to seek the Holy, which means responding to God's invitation: Come and See.[24]

Our access to modern conveniences and modes of travel do not have to distance us from kinship with the Celtic *peregrini*. As brothers and sisters in Christ, we automatically share a pilgrim-identity; we are but travelers here on earth, journeying in this land only temporarily. We do indeed long for the "place of our resurrection" along with our Celtic predecessors.

However, if we desire to go in search of the "place of our resurrec-tion," it only follows that our own death must occur first. This is illustrated through the sacrificial choices of the Celtic *peregrini* of old, who, seek-ing to embark upon a literal journey of faith, were willing to leave behind all that was dear to them in earthly terms to follow the calling of God. Though our own journeys may not be as colorful, the spiritual quest re-quires the same of us: to take seriously the example that another great *peregrini*, the Apostle Paul, set forth to the early church in Galatia:[25] "I have been crucified with Christ and I no longer live, but Christ lives in me. The life I live in the body, I live by faith in the Son of God, who loved me and gave himself for me" (Gal. 2:20).

Celtic Blessing

God the Father all-powerful, benign,
Jesu the Son of tears and of sorrow,
With thy co-assistance, O! Holy Spirit.
The Three-one, ever-living, ever-mighty,
    Everlasting,
Who brought the Children of Israel
    Through the Red Sea,
And Jonah to land from the belly of the
    Great creature of the ocean.
When the storm poured on the Sea of
    Galilee,
Sain us and shield and sanctify us,
Be Thou, King of the elements, seated at
    Our helm,
And lead us in peace to the end of our
    Journey.
With winds mild, kindly, benign,
    Pleasant,
Without swirl, without whirl, without
    Eddy,
That would do no harmful deed to us.
We ask all things of Thee, O God,
According to Thine own will and word.[26]

Meditation: Exodus 3:1-15

Note: Resist the temptation to believe that you already "know" this passage, this story. Patiently move through the Scripture and be open to the new thing the Spirit of God wants to show you.

Now Moses was tending the flock of Jethro his father-in-law, the priest of Midian, and he led the flock to the far side of the desert and came to

Horeb, the mountain of God. There the angel of the LORD appeared to him in flames of fire from within a bush. Moses saw that though the bush was on fire it did not burn up. So Moses thought, "I will go over and see this strange sight—why the bush does not burn up."

When the LORD saw that he had gone over to look, God called to him from within the bush, "Moses! Moses!" And Moses said, "Here I am."

"Do not come any closer," God said. "Take off your sandals, for the place where you are standing is holy ground." Then he said, "I am the God of your father, the God of Abraham, the God of Isaac and the God of Jacob." At this, Moses hid his face, because he was afraid to look at God.

The LORD said, "I have indeed seen the misery of my people in Egypt. I have heard them crying out because of their slave drivers, and I am concerned about their suffering. So I have come down to rescue them from the hand of the Egyptians and to bring them up out of that land into a good and spacious land, a land flowing with milk and honey—the home of the Canaanites, Hittites, Amorites, Perizzites, Hivites and Jebusites. And now the cry of the Israelites has reached me, and I have seen the way the Egyptians are oppressing them. So now, go. I am sending you to Pharaoh to bring my people the Israelites out of Egypt."

But Moses said to God, "Who am I, that I should go to Pharaoh and bring the Israelites out of Egypt?"

And God said, "I will be with you. And this will be the sign to you that it is I who have sent you: When you have brought the people out of Egypt, you will worship God on this mountain."

Moses said to God, "Suppose I go to the Israelites and say to them, 'The God of your fathers has sent me to you,' and they ask me, 'What is his name?' Then what shall I tell them?"

God said to Moses, "I AM WHO I AM. This is what you are to say to the Israelites: 'I AM has sent me to you.' "

God also said to Moses, "Say to the Israelites, 'The LORD, the God of your fathers—the God of Abraham, the God of Isaac and the God of Jacob— has sent me to you.' This is my name forever, the name by which I am to be remembered from generation to generation."

Reflection Questions

1. What are the journeys that are ahead for you: business travel? Family vacation? Other? Think through the different aspects of that future trip: the preparation/packing; the transportation process; the final destination; the people you will travel with; the people you will meet; your schedule; your return home. What can you do now to prepare yourself for a more meaningful journey?

2. Which of your friends or family have just returned from a journey? Make a point of asking them what their trip meant to them (as opposed to, "What did you do?")—how it changed them, how it forced them to think about life differently, how it led them to God. Commit to giving them your full attention, patiently waiting for them to get beyond "postcard news" onto the real issues of the inner journey.

3. As you reflect upon past journeys, great and small, where have been the "places of resurrection"?

FIVE

SILENCE AND SOLITUDE

From Chaos to Clarity

Iona Journal

Today I'm taking some time for silence and solitude, and I've chosen to spend it in the part of the Abbey sanctuary labeled the "Quiet Corner."

As I sit here, doing absolutely nothing but breathing the Jesus Prayer ("Lord Jesus Christ, Son of God, have mercy on me"), I realize that even with my T-shirt, long-sleeved shirt, grey fleece jacket, windbreaker and knitted scarf, I am still chilly in this ancient stone building. And I think about how at this same time my children and friends and co-workers in America are probably just getting ready for a busy day. Soon my girls will be up and about, gathering their books and backpacks, invariably one will be looking for socks, and, "Oh yeah, where's that permission slip that was supposed to be turned in yesterday?" I hope their dear grandparents are surviving it all. I think about the chapel service at the university, and what I would ordinarily be doing to prepare for it. It is a busy life, and I love it and am so grateful for it. Yet here I am *doing* nothing. "Lord Jesus Christ, Son of God, have mercy on me."

I look around in this Quiet Corner and take in its simplicity—the candle I lit earlier as I prayed for my friend and co-worker Carrie is still burning. (Carrie is fighting cancer. I'm stunned to remember that the last time I was on Iona, just three years ago, the candle I lit then was for her husband, Gary, who was going through his own bout of cancer.) On the small kneeling bench next to me Columba's Iona prophecy has been stitched in beautiful needlepoint, and carved on the side of it in Celtic lettering is the phrase, "In gratitude to God for many happy days." I hear the Iona Community choral group come into the Abbey to practice a rousing African tune, complete with tambourine and clapping. The mama sheep and their lambs grazing just outside the Abbey window have suddenly broken into a chorus of their own. And now I hear one of the Iona Community volunteers "hoovering" (vacuuming) in a nearby Abbey room. How did this blissful silence suddenly become so noisy?

In the midst of all this sudden activity, I am here doing nothing. I am not producing anything. I'm not even praying "big" prayers. The Jesus Prayer somehow seems to be complete and enough. I know that most of the world—most of the Christian world—has difficulty with the contemplative concept of being still, of taking our hands off of running the world for awhile and letting God be God. I have difficulty with that as well.

I take a moment to return to my daily pattern of reading short passages in the Gospel of Luke, which I've been doing for a few months now. My reading today has Jesus on the Mount of Olives, where he went "as usual" it says, to pray. *As usual.* Two pretty powerful words! This tells me that Jesus not only took that particular time to be alone and quiet with God, he apparently made it part of his routine. I know this is not the first time the text has mentioned that Jesus sought out solitude. But I certainly have never noticed that "as usual" in the same way that I do now.

This gives me a sense of God's approval. That this time of doing nothing and being nothing with him is good. The time will come soon enough when I will once again enter my busy life. I hope I will still be saying the Jesus Prayer as I do.

'This is what the Sovereign LORD, the Holy One of Israel, says:
'In repentance and rest is your salvation, in quietness and trust
is your strength, but you would have none of it.'"
Isaiah 30:15

In the previous chapter we discussed the Celtic practice of *peregrinatio*, and included in that discussion was a general distinction between being a tourist and being a pilgrim. A quick way of reviewing that difference might be to say that tourists bring back gifts and souvenirs from their journeys; pilgrims bring back intangible blessings.[1] Another way of understanding the distinction—again rather generally—might be to assess how one feels internally after the journeying—whether exhausted or renewed. *Renewal* most accurately describes the intended objective of a pilgrimage. If one is in search of "resurrection" on such a journey, it would only follow that new life should be the result.

Perhaps we should ask ourselves, what is it that gives us life? Are there practices, experiences, and resources that feed the deepest parts of our souls? If that is difficult to answer, perhaps it's because we are so often operating out of a state of fatigue—physically and, most especially, spiritually. Even the things we do in the name of "spirituality" or "Christian service" can drain us dry. "Burn-out" is a term we've grown familiar with as we observe depleted ministers, professionals, parents, all "good Christian folk." How is it that so much of the modern American (and I daresay "Christian") lifestyle is not, as a rule, a life-giving endeavor? After a full day of work, running the kids to baseball and ballet, driving through McDonalds, rushing to the church board meeting, then collapsing into bed, we can identify with the Teacher of Ecclesiastes: "'Meaningless! Meaningless! . . . Utterly meaningless! Everything is meaningless.' What does man gain from all his labor at which he toils under the sun?" (Eccles. 1:2, 3).

We are products of the "Protestant Work Ethic," and for all the good that this philosophy has done, a significant amount of curse comes with it. Yes, we are hard workers. Yes, we are productive. Yet our toil often leaves us feeling empty and unsatisfied. This malady cannot merely be attributed to the demon of "busyness"; we are not beset by meaninglessness simply because we are busy. We miss the meaning to be found in our lives because we ignore a principle that is as old as Creation itself: the intentional back and forth rhythm of work and rest.

In the early Celtic monastic settlements a sabbatical rhythm was in place. This was not only lived out through the once-a-week honoring of the sabbath. The Celts sanctified time so that each day, each week, each year demonstrated a rhythmic balance, what the Benedictines called *ora et labora*, "prayer and work."[2]

Part of this included a "rhythm of engagement in and withdrawal from the world."[3] Pilgrimage, as we saw earlier, was part of this rhythm. But the journeying, the actual traveling, was only the first part of that endeavor, the process of arriving at what they hoped would be the place of their resurrection where they would discover their truest and deepest selves in Christ. For such a transforming work to be complete, they believed they must seek solitude in the "desert."

Why the Desert?

Desert spirituality might be summed up in this classic charge, given by one of the Desert Fathers to his apprentice: "Go into your cell, and your cell will teach you everything." The Celts were inspired by the lives of the Egyptian desert fathers and mothers, and learned, through their examples, the spiritual disciplines of withdrawal—of solitude and silence —that trained them to re-engage their community more effectively. Of course the climate and landscape of Ireland and the British Isles was most un-desert-like. The Celts did what they could to replicate the desert experience, removing themselves from their ordinary life-sustaining resources—their communities, their supplies of food, their homes— seeking the place of their resurrection in locations far away from what was comfortable and familiar.

On Iona and in other locations across the UK and Ireland the remains of ancient hermitages can be found, evidence that the practice of seeking seclusion was taken seriously. Between the two high points on Iona lie the remains of such a hermitage: a mere ring of stones, 15 feet wide with the indication of a door to the southwest. These small huts were typically without windows, so such placement of a door would allow maximum exposure to afternoon sunlight.[4] While it is unlikely that this particular cell was used by Columba, a number of accounts tell of Columba seeking times of prayerful solitude at a variety of sacred locations around Iona.

What would it have been like to have spent days or weeks inside a hut made of stone? We can engage our imaginations a bit to try to get the sense of it. A dirt floor for a bed. Maybe a stone for a pillow, as Columba himself supposedly used. Perhaps a candle or oil lamp would be used in the evening when it was time for a simple meal. And during the day, the doorway would serve as the solitary source of light—that is, if the sun was shining. On dreary, misty days in the Western Hebrides, there would be precious little light, making it very difficult to read whatever materials one might be fortunate enough to have, the Scriptures themselves were a rare commodity. Surely the wind would howl and whistle through the cracks in the stone walls, interrupting one's silence with the lonely sounds of winter and its chill. In the summer the air would be thick and humid with warmer temperatures and very little circulation to refresh the solitary soul inside.

The tradition of monks building small huts or stone cells for the purpose of retreat continued long after the time of Columba.[5] They removed themselves from action—from work and from speaking—to be reminded that in the end it is the action of God that propels one forward toward Christlikeness. They even utilized the terminology of the desert, naming their places of hermitage "Dysart" or "Disserth," both of which are derived from the word "desert."[6] These terms remain on some of our modern maps today, hearkening back to ancient times when faithful pilgrims sought the place of resurrection.

Desert imagery isn't new to us "word-centered" evangelicals. We can easily think of the variety of instances where God used the desert as a place of transformation for his people at large or for individuals. Moses and the children of Israel encountered God in the desert, and through that encounter we receive a profound image of God's promise of redemption and deliverance. John the Baptist preached his message of repentance out in the wilderness margins of civilization, sacramentally "burying" people in baptism so they could be raised to new life.

Jesus Christ himself had his own desert experience, having been sent out into the desert, not by Satan, but by the Holy Spirit, for forty days of fasting from food and the demands of earthly life (Matt. 4; Mark 1; Luke 4). Here we see Jesus in God's training program, fighting off the temptations of the Evil One in preparation not only for ministry, but for the ultimate battle of the will that he would face in Gethsemane.

Celtic Hermits

A bit of effort may be required to combat the untamed, counter-cultural image that the word "hermit" conjures up in our minds. While the stories of some of the Celtic hermits are colorful indeed, it is helpful to remember that the purpose for their seclusion was not merely to escape from the world, but to more fully engage with God. Michael Mitton writes,

> The Celtic church knew that prayer and devotion to God had to be at the heart of its life if it was effectively to witness to God. The hermit was to some degree living out fully what most Christians could live out only partially. It was essential that some from the community lived out this life for the sake of the community, and indeed for the sake of the wider community. The hermit provided a kind of anchor for a church which could easily have become over-busy, and which was no doubt tempted by materialism in much the same ways that the church is today.[7]

It is also important for us to remember that these hermits participated in the back and forth rhythm of prayer and work, of disengagement and engagement. As Mitton implies, very few chose seclusion as a permanent lifestyle, for their foundational commitment to communal living ran through their veins. Their ancestors passed on to them that Celtic clannish loyalty, which with the coming of the Gospel, was fanned into a fiery love for the Body of Christ, the communion of believers. Time away in solitude was primarily seen as preparation for re-entry into communal life, to experience newer vistas of worship and service.

Ian Bradley elaborates:

> Columba alternated periods of intense activity, running his large and complex monastic *familia* from Iona and dabbling in the politics of his native Ireland, with months of solitude on the island of Hinba. Cuthbert withdrew periodically from the frantic business of running the community at Lindisfarne and retreating with Northumbrian kings and princes to his hermit cell on the uninhabited Farne islands. In Wales, Dyfrig regularly retreated from the busy monastery at Llantwit Major to Caldy Island.[8]

A classic example of the Celtic hermit is found in St. Kevin of Glendalough (498-618). Legendary stories about St. Kevin have been passed down through many Celtic generations. The earliest account of Kevin was not written until five hundred years after his death,[9] so we have to take these stories with a pretty substantial grain of salt. However, stories, as we know, can be profound agents of truth and instruction. While they may seem rather outlandish, it is through these accounts of Kevin's life that we can observe this rhythm of work and prayer, of community and solitude, of engagement and silence.

Colorful adjectives may be used to describe this Celtic saint: mystic, hermit, abbot, miracle worker. At the Upper Lake of Glendalough, south of what is now Dublin, Kevin made his hermitage, staying for many days alone in silent fellowship with God and creation. He eventually founded the great monastery at Glendalough, and it became a thriving "city" of prayer, study, service, and worship. Yet for Kevin, the call to solitude and silence remained in his heart, for he eventually commissioned his fellow monks to lead the monastery and left for the Upper Valley, just a

mile from the monastery, to create his hermitage. There he lived in com-
plete solitude for four years, perhaps longer. Michael Rodgers and Marcus
Losack, Catholic and Anglican priests, respectively, who currently live at
Glendalough, provide helpful commentary:

> The experience of prayer and austerity, instead of harden-
> ing Kevin, enabled him to express his gentleness and become
> more at one with himself, with creation and with God. He lived
> in a place beneath the cliffs on the shores of the Upper Lake,
> which remains in shadow for at least six months of the year.
> The reality of this must be woven through our understanding
> of Kevin's life at this time. It is also a very beautiful place, where
> even today there is a great atmosphere of peace and seclusion.
> It was here that Kevin's desire for solitude was realized, and he
> developed close relationships with even the wildest animals.[10]

One of the more fantastic and well-known stories of Kevin shows
him praying, as many of the Celtic saints did, in "cross vigil," meaning that
he stood or knelt with "arms out-stretched in the shape of a cross (the
sacred tree)."[11] Praying this way, in such a tiny cell, required that his arms
would stretch out the window of his tiny dwelling. It was there, during
Kevin's prayer, that a blackbird came to build a nest in his open hand. The
story claims that Kevin, aware that the bird had laid an egg in her new
nest, remained in the cross vigil position for days, perhaps weeks, until
the baby bird was hatched.[12]

What an illustration of what happens when one finds the place of resurrection! This legend of Kevin may first of all remind us of the vigilance
and sacrifice of Christ himself, enduring the pain of the cross so that we
might be raised to new life. It also can metaphorically illustrate the process of our own spiritual transformation, that to become new creatures
in Christ is a very slow but beautiful process, one that requires stillness
and patient waiting.

Conversely, Kevin's seeming lack of action in this situation might
actually make us nervous. I find myself thinking, "Kevin! Just find a nice

place for that nest, put it down and move on! Put your multi-tasking skills to work, man!" That's certainly what I would have felt compelled to do had I been in his position.

Yet there seems to be something inherently formative in Kevin's *act of not-acting*—his willingness to remain motionless so that new life can arise. It counters our modern-day Christian sensibilities that put so much emphasis on *doing*. It presents a radical new paradigm, one that's actually not new at all, for the biblical Teacher of Ecclesiastes himself arrived at a conclusion that addresses this problem. He proclaimed that there is a time to plant and a time to reap. But what do we do when we're doing neither? *We wait and watch the plant grow.* There is little else we can do in that seemingly unproductive time of waiting for God to bring forth new life. The implied truth is: *There is a time to do nothing.* "There remains, then, a Sabbath-rest for the people of God; for anyone who enters God's rest also rests from his own work, just as God did from his" (Heb. 4:9-10).

This is a great reversal of modern-day values. I succumb to those modern values myself when I believe that every moment of my day must be productive, that I must have something to show for my time. Yet clearly, biblical wisdom and the Celtic example relieve us of this compulsion, saying, in effect, "Don't just do something, *stand there*!"

Contemporary Practice

It is important to remember here that this is a *spiritual discipline* we're talking about, a way of training in godliness, not just a "get out of work free" ticket. Solitude is actually extremely productive; the difference is that it is not we who are doing the work, but the Holy Spirit of God in us. We take our hands off so he can do the transforming work. Resurrection is always his doing. Rightly defined, solitude is "the creation of an open, empty space in our lives by purposefully abstaining from interaction with other human beings, so that, freed from competing loyalties, we can be found by God."[13]

Henri Nouwen is one author (among many, both classic and contemporary) that has helped me understand the disciplines of silence and solitude. His book *The Way of the Heart* proclaims that all of our *doing* for Christ means little without intentional time of *being with* Christ.

Nouwen shows us that what really happens in solitude is the death of what he calls our "false self"—the self that is determined by external image and illusion. Our instinct is to cover ourselves, Adam-like, with the externalities of title, possessions, and achievement, making it much easier to ignore the true state of our souls. In solitude we are forced to set aside these external trappings and allow God to put to death what is false and superficial about us in order to raise the "new self" created in the image and likeness of Christ.

To truly be free of this false self, we can take a cue from the Celtic hermit. "Without solitude we remain victims of our society and continue to be entangled in the illusions of the false self."[14] Retreating for a period of time from ringing phones, burgeoning email boxes, to-do lists, and obligations gives God some space to do what he wants to do with us. It helps us remember that the Sabbath was meant to be a day of rest, a time to step away from all that convinces us that we are indispensable to the world and to be assured that we are in the hands of God.

That familiar verse in Psalm 46:10, "Be still, and know that I am God" is often printed on all manner of Christian paraphernalia as a soothing devotional accent. It is indeed a compelling thought, but it is incomplete without the context of the entire psalm. Here we see that God is not merely inviting us into a blissful reverie, but is rather giving us a stern reminder. "Cease striving," the New American Standard translation says. Or, in my own words, "Stop—I am God, and you are not! Put this in perspective! You, Tracy, are not in charge of this world—let go and know that I am managing things. *Just stop for awhile.*"

I heard a story recently about an English-speaking pastor who was preaching on this passage in Japan, and when the Japanese translator communicated it to Japanese listeners, he translated it, "Lay down your weapons." Doesn't this speak to the ways we defend ourselves, hiding behind the illusion of control?

No Space

My friend Becci and I were killing time in a London airport gift shop a few years ago when we came upon a delightful tome of pessimistic, practical wisdom, *Eeyore's Little Book of Gloom*. Its contents sent the two of us into spasms of laughter, as it was so completely the opposite of the fluffy, feel-good books one typically finds in gift shops. (Reading it aloud in a languid, quasi-bass voice also helped.) An example: "You can give the donkey a happy ending . . . but the miserable beginning remains forever." And, under the title "Accentuate the Negative," Eeyore bemoans, "We can't all, and some of us don't. That's all there is to it. . . . I'm not complaining, but There It Is."

Easy for me to laugh; I don't have to go through life with my tail thumb-tacked on. But I do have a wee bit of misery of my own that enjoys Eeyore's company, particularly as illustrated in the following excerpt entitled, "Leave Them Wanting Less":

Everybody crowds round so in this Forest. There's no Space. I never saw a more Spreading lot of animals in my life, and all in the wrong places. Can't you *see* that Christopher Robin wants to be alone?[15]

The fact is, I need a little space now and then. My world gets too crowded with noise and activity. God's voice is barely a squeak in the midst of it, because apparently there is a "Spreading lot of animals" filling up my life. Eeyore is right: "There's no Space."

I also see this in the lives of the university students I work with. They are extremely productive, but in their crowded lives they, too, find it difficult to hear God. So, twice a semester, I take groups of them away for the day for a mini silent retreat. They submit (reluctantly, at first) to an afternoon of no talking and no iPods, away from perfectionism and the stress of relationships, away from the "animals" that are "all in the wrong places." We sit alone. We pray in silence. We listen for the whispers of the Holy Spirit through his Word. We make space for God. The psalmist illustrates this well:

Lift up your heads, O you gates;
be lifted up, you ancient doors,
that the King of glory may come in. (Ps. 24:7)

In doing so, we discover the kind of joy that comes when the obstacles are removed and the Holy Spirit of God is once again allowed to roam freely in and through us.

Retreating

I find it somewhat interesting how our Christian understanding of "retreat" has come to be rather limited in its scope. Growing up in the evangelical context, I've attended numerous retreats. The opportunity to have a weekend away from the demands of work and family, to be with friends and hear a stimulating speaker is generally pretty appealing to most of us. Yet most of these "retreats" offer very little in the way of Sabbath rest. Somehow we've come to believe that a retreat must be packed full of stimulating activities—dynamic speakers, mixer games, activities, excursions, discussions. Even in our retreating we are not given permission to cease activity. It's curious how we keep managing to push that Fourth Commandment aside.

Now these kinds of events are enjoyable and have their place in our lives. I myself plan one or two of them every year for our students. Getaways like this can be good for the soul in some ways, but they are not truly retreats. For instead of removing us from our normal level of activity, they merely replace it with different activity. If we are to appropriate a Sabbath rhythm in our lives, these kinds of events cannot stand alone as the sole provider of a retreat experience.

Real Ideas

We have, indeed, to fashion our own desert where we can withdraw every day, shake off our compulsions, and dwell in the gentle healing presence of our Lord. Without such a desert we will lose our own soul while preaching the gospel to others.

But with such a spiritual abode, we will become increasingly conformed to him in whose Name we minister.[16]

I greatly appreciate a local church in our town, whose leadership had the vision a number of years ago to create a prayer trail on the wooded property of their church. In addition to the trail, they have built two "prayer cottages" that are available for a small donation to be used by individuals for prayerful solitude. They allow anyone to come and use this facility, and I have gladly taken them up on the offer a number of times. To take a day to be alone with God in such a beautiful setting renews my soul in an extraordinary way. The "hermitage" they have created there provides a place for me to discover my truest self in God and experience a life-giving place of resurrection.

This church's ministry strikes me as profoundly counter-cultural. By creating this marvelous environment where God can do his transforming work, this church is saying to their congregation and to the world, "Cease striving! Let God be God in your life! Stop all the 'doing' and let God do it!" This church makes it possible to resist the "chasing after the wind" of Ecclesiastes, choosing instead to wait in stillness for the moving of the holy wind of the Spirit of God.

Richard Foster demonstrates that finding ways of observing Sabbath, of incorporating the disciplines of silence and solitude, is easier than we might think. He offers these helpful suggestions:

> Take a pre-dawn walk, listening to the awakening sounds of your world (whether city or country). Limit your speaking for one day and see what you learn about yourself and others. Sit in an airport or bus station and observe people carefully, reflecting on what you see. Take a one-day silent retreat—or a three-day retreat, a seven-day retreat. . . . For one month leave your car radio off and make your morning commute a mini-retreat. Arise at 2:00 a.m., light a single candle as a reminder of the presence of Christ, and for one hour listen to the sounds

of the night. You will, I am sure, think of many more ways to discover wilderness time for yourself.[17]

Information vs. Transformation

Many of us in the evangelical tradition have been greatly formed through Bible study. All of that reading with our heads—for *information*—helps us think clearly and rightly about important theological issues. Monastic life most certainly included the intentional study of Scripture.

However, reading with our hearts—for *transformation*—calls for a different and equally necessary approach. This particular approach to Scripture, called *lectio divina,* "sacred reading," is not exclusively Celtic, but it is an accurate representation of the ancient European monastic approach to meditating upon Scripture. It is based upon the daily, rhythmic reading and recitation of the Psalms, which the Celtic Christians heartily embraced.

The meditative process of *lectio divina* is itself quite simple. What is difficult is reorienting our disposition when coming to the Scripture, so attached are we to the task of fact-finding and filling in the blanks. In *lectio divina* we adopt a quiet posture that is slow-moving, with no expectation to accomplish or produce anything (that is the Holy Spirit's job). We must lay aside our compulsion to "get through" the Scripture. We must resist the temptation to apply any type of study paradigm—diligent hunting for facts is not allowed. And we who are teachers and pastors need to cast aside that ever-present need to turn Scripture into a great lesson or sermon!

The term *lectio* is given to the first step in the process, *lectio* meaning "to read." I call it the "ingest" stage. We begin by selecting a small passage of Scripture—a story from the Gospels, a psalm, or a short episode from the Old Testament—and then deliberately reading it slowly, refusing to give in to our compulsion to get through the passage quickly.

The term *meditatio,* meaning "to meditate," is given to the next step. I call it the "digest" stage. We read the same passage slowly again, savoring it, allowing it to move from our minds to our hearts. It truly is a sort of digestive process, because by digesting it we want this Word to become part of us. Think of a cow chewing on its cud, slowly, deliberately, repeatedly, and you've got a picture of *meditatio*. My friend Jan Johnson says that if you know how to worry, you know how to meditate!

> When we worry, we ask, "What if (this terrible thing) happens?" And we rehash all the awful possibilities. When we meditate, we focus on a Scripture and ask, "What if I had been the person Jesus healed? What would that experience have been like?" Entering the text this way retrains the soul by helping us encounter God in a personal way and live in the sense that we have been spoken to personally by God. The stunning result of these encounters with God is that our natural tendencies to be self-centered are overridden by the desire to please the God we have just encountered.[18]

The term *oratio*, meaning "to speak," is assigned to the third step. I call it the "request" stage, for while reading the passage yet again, we begin to ask the Holy Spirit, "What is it that I am to do in response to this Scripture? What is it that you want me to see here?" Yes, it apparently takes three times (maybe more!) of reading the passage before we are ready to receive the answer to this question.

And finally *contemplatio*, meaning "to contemplate." I call this the "rest" stage, for while slowly reading the passage a final time, we are resting in God's love and mercy for us, trusting that the Scripture has moved from head to heart and that God will complete his transforming work in us.

The implication here is not to reject "head" knowledge. The Celtic Christians greatly valued the discipline of learning and critical thinking, as we will see in an upcoming chapter. Our typical, information-gathering approach to Scripture must not be completely abandoned. The discipline of *lectio divina*, of sacred reading, provides a proper meditative balance to an informational approach to Scripture, taking us closer to the rhythm of work and prayer that we see modeled in monastic life. To come to the

Scriptures with the same sort of sabbatical attitude of ceasing from our work, of resting, of waiting, makes us receptive to the truth of God in ways that are inaccessible to us when we are decidedly "in charge."

The Sound of Sheer Silence

Lectio divina not only gives us a way to "cease striving" in our approach to Scripture; it also is a discipline that nurtures the interior skill of listening to the voice of God. This concept is often illustrated with the story of Elijah, as found in 1 Kings 19. This is yet another in the collection of biblical narratives that demonstrate the life transformation that comes by way of the desert. The New Revised Standard Version says that God got Elijah's attention through the "sound of sheer silence" (1 Kings 19:12). How can there be sound *in silence?* For Elijah and all of us who seek after the voice of God, silence isn't truly silent after all.

The practice of silence is illustrated in Geoffrey Moorehouse's historical novel, *Sun Dancing.* The author relates pieces of wisdom from a fictional Celtic *anamchara* to his monk apprentice:

> You must simply open yourself to God's grace, by excluding everything that might come between you and Him. Open yourself and be still. Nothing in this life is more important than the stillness of it. We are, all of us, on this *skeilic* ("sharp rock") because there is a stillness here we have not found anywhere else, and in that stillness we must listen, listen, listen. Be still and listen, my little brother. Open yourself and be still and breathe the prayer. Trust that the Lord will then raise you up. . . . There is no other way."[19]

The Celts knew what it was to have a "listening life," to be attentive to the voice and movement of the Spirit through all things, at all times. Whether we are in sacred places like Iona, or in a silent cathedral, on a mountain path, or on our morning commute, we can begin to understand how this listening posture might be possible—because we are away from all of the noise, all of the voices that not only draw us away from

the pure voice of God, but that try to convince us that they are the voices
worth listening to.

Perhaps we should consider when we last experienced true silence.
It may be difficult for us to say with any accuracy, because we've gotten so
used to the hum of electronic devices around us that we don't even realize
that we live with a constant level of noise. This fact came to my attention
one afternoon when we lost electricity in my office building. The lack of
whirring from copiers, printers, computers, even light fixtures left us with a
shocking void of sound. When did I last drive in my car without the stereo
playing? When was the last time my family and I sat around the dinner
table with phones, dishwasher, and television turned off? None of these
things are evil. But could it be that the many layers of noise we dwell in have
numbed our sensitivity to the still small voice of God? "The more the words,
the less the meaning, and how does that profit anyone?" (Eccles. 6:11).

Then there is the *interior* noise that confronts us each day. Even when
we finally arrive at a physical place of solitude, far from the noise of daily
life, the noises of our own minds and hearts grow ever louder, making it
much more difficult to be alone and still than we might have predicted.
The external noise may have been completely eliminated, yet internally
we experience a cacophonous collection of worries and mental images
that threaten to keep us from the still and peaceful presence of the Spirit
of God. C.S. Lewis likens this universal experience of interior noise to being stampeded by a charging herd of wild animals (I think he and Eeyore
got together on that one).

Whenever I take students on silent retreat, each time, without fail,
there is the complaint among us about how difficult it is to be still because
of the riot of thoughts that chaotically parade across our consciousness.
Is there any help for us in this frustrating condition? My guess is that our
early Celtic forebears experienced the same kinds of frustrations. The fact
that they spent extended periods of time in silence and solitude may hint
at a truth we don't want to accept: being still before God takes practice.

What is ultimately true about this is that noise—either its presence or
absence—is a significant factor in our spiritual formation. Because what

we listen to is what we become. This is why the meditative approach to Scripture, through practices like *lectio divina*, is so essential in the process of becoming Christlike. Psalm 1 paints a vivid and appealing picture of the results of meditation in our lives, explaining that the man or woman who meditates on the Word of God day and night will thrive and flourish like a verdant tree by the water's edge, "which yields its fruit in season and whose leaf does not wither. Whatever he does prospers" (Ps. 1:3).

We ingest and digest the Word of God, following Jesus' example, who, in the desert, proclaimed that it is our only true nourishment. Conversely, if our attention is constantly turned to the humanly created, distracting noise of life, we will be shaped accordingly. "Listen to advice and accept instruction, and in the end you will be wise" (Prov. 19:20).

A few years ago I led a group of 19 women on a pilgrimage to Iona. Because this would be such a new experience for them, I was a bit fearful that after six days on a tiny island they might begin to feel stuck, claustrophobic, antsy. We would not have a television accessible to us. There were no phones in the hotel rooms, nor did our cell phones operate from there. There is no "town center" on Iona for long days of shopping, only the quaint village with shops whose contents could easily be exhausted in a single afternoon. Life on Iona is so relaxed that there is not even a police force; I knew that we wouldn't even have keys to lock our hotel rooms. I worried that in light of all of that "nothingness" they would regret making the significant financial sacrifice that international travel requires. So in response to my fears, I threw in a couple of days of sight-seeing in spectacular Edinburgh, hoping that would appease anyone eager to get back to "the real world."

How astonished I was to later learn that by the end of our journey many of them wished we had taken *more* time on Iona! Edinburgh—while enjoyable, fascinating, and one of the most beautiful cities in Europe— proved unnecessary for many of them. They had found their sanctuary, some space for God on Iona, a place of resurrection.

And to think that some of us believe that God commanded a Sabbath rest just so we'd have a day to go to church! Yes, our corporate worship time is essential. But through these disciplines of silence and solitude we're discovering that Sabbath is so much more. It is a day, a time, a discipline where God meets us and raises us and makes us into the image of his Son.

A psalmist named Asaph found this to be profoundly true, and he shares his findings with us in Psalm 73. Here we are invited into Asaph's worldview, one that initially concluded that living the life of faith is utterly futile, and in the end, totally pointless. He comes to this conclusion because he sees all around him the "good life" of those who, though living in wickedness and licentiousness, seem to prosper and be blessed:

> . . . I envied the arrogant
>> when I saw the prosperity of the wicked.
> They have no struggles;
>> their bodies are healthy and strong.
> They are free from the burdens common to man;
>> they are not plagued by human ills.

Meanwhile, Asaph tries to live faithfully before God, and what does he get for it?

> Surely in vain have I kept my heart pure;
> in vain have I washed my hands in innocence.
> All day long I have been plagued;
> I have been punished every morning.

When Asaph looks around, he can only conclude that those who choose a selfish, godless life actually make out better in the end. Just about the time that Asaph jettisons it all, the psalm pivots from one horizon to the other—he enters the "sanctuary of God" (vs. 17). It is in the sanctuary where Asaph tells us he began to understand, to see clearly; he has an incredible "aha!" experience. In the presence of an all-wise God, the prosperity of the "rich and famous" melt into oblivion, and Asaph comes away with the certainty that God is enough for him:

> Whom have I in heaven but you?
> And earth has nothing I desire besides you.

> *My flesh and my heart may fail,*
> *but God is the strength of my heart*
> *and my portion forever.*
> *Those who are far from you will perish;*
> *you destroy all who are unfaithful to you.*
> *But as for me, it is good to be near God.*
> *I have made the Sovereign LORD my refuge;*
> *I will tell of all your deeds.*

In the cell of silence and solitude, this is the essential kernel of truth that is heard: when all is said and done, *it is good to be near God.* By removing the noise and external clutter for periodic entry into the "sanctuary," into the very conscious presence of God, we make ourselves available to gain a completely different perspective, a life-giving rule that equips us to live in an obsessive, materialistic world.

From Selfishness to Selflessness

Does this ring True?

Ironically, it is through solitude—through intentional times being alone with God only—that we are transformed into people who demonstrate compassion to others. This is why the desert fathers and mothers and the Celtic hermits were so often sought out as spiritual advisors, as *anamchara*, to others. Their time spent in solitude with God resulted in a greater capacity for physical hospitality and spiritual friendship. Such transformation happens when we let go of the outward manifestations of the "false self," which take so much energy to maintain. Our will and our way is relinquished so that God's will and way may be had in us; and the result in that transaction is always the humility and compassion of Christ in us. Here we see yet another way to identify with Christ in his suffering, for in a time of intense solitude he too was asked to relinquish his own will that God's might be done, (Luke 22:42). "Thus in and through solitude we do not move away from people. On the contrary, we move closer to them through compassionate ministry."[20]

   Nouwen affirms what the Celts and many believers since have known to be true, that "solitude is the furnace of transformation."[21] Sabbath is not only given to us so we can enjoy physical rest, but it is primarily given to us for *spiritual* rest and renewal. When we intentionally remove ourselves from earthly trappings, we are forced to face up to our own nothingness, drawing us to "surrender ourselves totally and unconditionally to the Lord Jesus Christ."[22] Here is where we can begin to become our truest, deepest selves in Christ—the kind of people he wants doing his kingdom work in a world he desperately loves.

Celtic Blessing

I wish, O Son of the living God,
eternal, ancient King,
for a secret hut in the wilderness
that it may be my dwelling.

A very blue shallow well
to be beside it,
a clear pool for washing away sins
through the grace of the Holy Ghost.

A beautiful wood close by
around it on every side
for the nurture of many-voiced birds
to shelter and hide it.

Facing the south for warmth
a little stream across its ground,
a choice plot with abundant bounties
which would be good for every plant. . . .

This is the house keeping I would get,
I would choose it without concealing,

fragrant fresh leeks, hens,
salmon, trout, bees.

My fill of clothing and food
from the King of good fame,
and for me to be sitting for a time
praying to God in every place.[23]

Meditation: 1 Kings 19:1-13

Now Ahab told Jezebel everything Elijah had done and how he had killed all the prophets with the sword. So Jezebel sent a messenger to Elijah to say, "May the gods deal with me, be it ever so severely, if by this time tomorrow I do not make your life like that of one of them."

Elijah was afraid and ran for his life. When he came to Beersheba in Judah, he left his servant there, while he himself went a day's journey into the desert. He came to a broom tree, sat down under it and prayed that he might die. "I have had enough, LORD," he said. "Take my life; I am no better than my ancestors." Then he lay down under the tree and fell asleep.

All at once an angel touched him and said, "Get up and eat." He looked around, and there by his head was a cake of bread baked over hot coals, and a jar of water. He ate and drank and then lay down again.

The angel of the LORD came back a second time and touched him and said, "Get up and eat, for the journey is too much for you." So he got up and ate and drank. Strengthened by that food, he traveled forty days and forty nights until he reached Horeb, the mountain of God. There he went into a cave and spent the night.

And the word of the LORD came to him: "What are you doing here, Elijah?"

He replied, "I have been very zealous for the LORD God Almighty. The Israelites have rejected your covenant, broken down your altars, and put your prophets to death with the sword. I am the only one left, and now they are trying to kill me too."

The LORD said, "Go out and stand on the mountain in the presence of the LORD, for the LORD is about to pass by."

Then a great and powerful wind tore the mountains apart and shattered the rocks before the LORD, but the LORD was not in the wind. After the wind there was an earthquake, but the LORD was not in the earthquake. After the earthquake came a fire, but the LORD was not in the fire. And after the fire came a gentle whisper. When Elijah heard it, he pulled his cloak over his face and went out and stood at the mouth of the cave.

Then a voice said to him, "What are you doing here, Elijah?"

Reflection Questions

1. Have you ever heard God speak to you through the sound of "sheer silence"? How did you know that it was the voice of God?

2. What other voices are competing for your attention right now? What can you do to "turn down the volume" on the ones that are drawing you away from God?

3. Where is your favorite place to meet with God? Consider a place in your home, a nearby church, or a place outdoors that you could make into a "cell."

SIX

SAINTS AND SYMBOLS

From Visible to Invisible

Iona Journal

The Iona Community is an intriguing group, living, working, worshiping together according to a daily rhythm that may not be very different from the Benedictine community that thrived on Iona from around 1200 to 1500, and perhaps not too different from the Columban monastic community's rhythm of life as they lived here between 563 and around 900. (Those dates are unreal to me, not only because it's difficult to grasp how many years have passed between the days of Columba and the days of Me—but because those ancient believers seem strangely real, close in a way. The centuries disappear in light of our fellowship in Christ.)

I have watched the Iona Community members with curiosity. The other day I walked through the sanctuary of the Abbey toward the gift shop on the other side of the cloisters, and I passed a community member sweeping the Abbey, and another polishing the wooden pews. I saw three more smiling Iona community members working in the Abbey gift shop. Even as I made the necessary "pit stop" on my way out, there in the restroom was another community volunteer dutifully cleaning.

It strikes me that the Iona Community is truly a praying community—praying through the usual activities of worship services and prayer groups.

But they also pray with their lives through acts of service, clearing the way for visitors, like me, to come and be with God in a significant way.

Off to the left side of the Abbey sanctuary is a room displaying the various social and humanitarian concerns that the Iona Community supports, telling me that they pray not only through simple tasks here on Iona, but also by working in the world for righteousness, mercy and justice in the name of Christ. I can't help but think that Columba and all those early Celtic believers who once lived and prayed on this island would be pleased that their legacy continues in this way.

I've also been very impressed at the thoughtfulness and intentionality of the worship services on Iona, led each morning and evening by members of the Community. Last night's service was a eucharistic service, full of symbolism and meaning. Upon entering the Abbey we were struck by the presence of a great long table, draped with a white tablecloth, set right in the middle of the sanctuary, running lengthwise down the aisle. Worshipers were actually sitting all around it as if coming to have dinner. The rest of us (the latecomers) occupied the choir seats on either side and continued in rows around the table. There were many candles lit on the table itself, as well as the usual candelabra all around, which gave the Abbey its familiar evening glow. Again I found it assuring to look around at the faces present and recognize fellow travelers. How absolutely incredible that, after a day of hoofing around the island, we were now all there together to receive the broken body and spilled blood of Christ!

The leader directed our attention to various articles on the communion table that represented resurrection and new life. I could see flowers scattered about on the table, and in the center, a standing cross that was fully covered in daffodils. As I thought about resurrection, I remembered that the Abbey tour guide told us earlier today that the snakes carved in the elaborately decorated St. Martin's Cross which stands outside of the Abbey were symbols of resurrection—because they shed their skin.

When it came time for the invitation to the Lord's Supper, our leader carefully reminded us about Christ's broken body represented by the bread and wine. Such powerful imagery! And as we all passed the peace in our wide variety of dialects—Polish, Canadian, African, Scottish, American—I was once again overwhelmed with the reality of that broken body for each of us: those standing around me as well as those whose ancient footprints we were standing on.

⚜

"For since the creation of the world
God's invisible qualities—his eternal power and divine nature—
have been clearly seen, being understood from what
has been made, so that men are without excuse."
Romans 1:20

Let's imagine that we've been given a challenge, and it is this: If we could choose just two physical, material objects to represent our truest selves, what two objects would do the trick? If we were to try to communicate some of the deepest, most important things about ourselves, what would we use?

I presented this challenge to a group of fellow educators at a seminar recently. One young woman explained one of her choices to us: a cell phone. The phone, she said, represents all of the important people in her life with whom she makes a special effort to stay in contact. She is a commuter, so while she's traveling back and forth in her car, she uses that time to connect, by phone, to her friends and family, and those relationships are of utmost importance to her.

Another gentleman described a painting of Jesus that is an important part of his family history. This particular painting contains the written words of the entire New Testament, written deftly within the illustrated body of Jesus. My colleague explained that he too wanted to embody the Word of God, just as this painting illustrated.

I loved hearing about the symbols that these class members had chosen because they helped us see something about each of them that we wouldn't otherwise be able to see. We know that Jesus gave us two physical objects that would always remind us of the deepest, truest aspects of himself: bread and wine, reminders of his sacrificial life and death. Throughout the Christian world these sacraments are recognized as "outward and visible signs of an inward and invisible grace." When we celebrate the Lord's Supper, we re-member Jesus (as opposed to dis-member). We do, in a sense, put him back together in our midst, corporately experiencing a deep love that is broken, spilled, and raised to new life.

The faith expression of the early Christian Celts was, at its core, sacramental in nature. As we saw in our discussion of their very ordinary ways of praying, every aspect of life presented to them an occasion for connection with God—a reason to pray, to listen, to worship, to exult, to delight in the goodness and nearness of God. We've seen in the Celtic appreciation of thin places that these early Christians were convinced that God is, indeed, very near to us and that nearness is sometimes sensed in unusual ways as physical locations become conduits of his Presence. Through the faith expression of these Celtic Christians, we see that all of life is sacred and covered with the fingerprints of God.

I remember one of the first times I was made aware of an outward sign of an invisible grace. It was in my elementary school years and Mrs. St. Clair was a neighbor friend of ours. She was an energetic, charismatic Christian woman, one who easily and enthusiastically proclaimed the glories of God. One day we were outdoors with Mrs. St. Clair when she called me over to take a look at something she'd picked up from the ground. It was a small twig from the cottonwood trees that populated our neighborhood. "I want to show you something," she said, and she proceeded to cleanly break that small twig in two, dividing it right down the middle of one of its knobby knuckles. I peered inside the cross-section of the twig. "Look," Mrs. St. Clair invited with delight. "See how much God loves you?" I marveled at the perfect brown star that was revealed in the center of that twig. "He made this just for you."

That image was a simple demonstration of God's creative love, unveiled by a woman who knew a teachable moment when she saw one. A twig would certainly not be recognized as a sacrament by any Christian denomination. Yet it most definitely revealed something invisible to me in a sacramental way. A truth of God was revealed and underlined through something as rudimentary as a twig.

Christians in early Ireland and Scotland used their prayerful imaginations and their artistic sensibilities to creatively communicate the truths of the Gospel. Since they seemed to have been determined to see the glory of God in all times and places, it follows that their own worship would be filled with image and symbolism. This is, of course, not unique to the Celts, but their own particular expression of this sacramental way of life certainly had a distinctive use and appearance all its own.

While Irish folklore loves to portray St. Patrick teaching about the Trinity by way of the three-leafed shamrock, experts have relegated it to the realm of legend. However, with even a cursory examination of some of the more widespread symbols of Celtic faith—the Celtic cross and the Celtic knot—we can see that such objects truly were and are aids to worship and, particularly in the case of the Celtic Cross, visible objects that reveal invisible truths.

The Cross

This symbol, the Celtic High Cross, may be the most widely recognized symbol of the Celtic Christian tradition. These fine exhibits of faith and artistry dot the Celtic landscape, but the greatest concentration can be found in Ireland "where more than sixty still remain largely intact."[1] Our brief encounter with these crosses in the chapter on thin places serves as a basic introduction to their significance. But there is a great deal more depth and meaning in these ancient Christian symbols that calls for our attention.

As members of a highly materialistic culture, it can be a challenge for us to grasp the significance these crosses held over a thousand years ago. Today we see a popular rapper on a music video displaying a large gold cross around his neck while spouting lyrics that blaspheme the Crucified. Crosses are easily obtained and viewed in all manner of holy and unholy locations. We don't need to take time here to elaborate on all of the ways the cross is misused in our culture; it's familiar enough to each of us without elaborating.

How different it was in early seventh century Ireland. Previous to that time, the cross was not a visible symbol of early Christianity, as "the idea that Jesus had suffered and died on the cross was unpalatable, especially since it was a cruel form of torturous death normally reserved for slaves."[2] When Jerusalem was sacked by the Persians in 613, it was believed that they took the "True Cross," the cross on which Jesus had actually been crucified. The Byzantine Emperor Heraclius reclaimed the True Cross, and it ushered in a new era of symbolic reverence of the cross. Irish monastic communities then began to be marked with the symbol of the cross, at first very simply with crosses carved on stones. By the ninth century, the artistry of the carved High Crosses was in full swing.

The presence of these crosses served a variety of spiritual and practical purposes. Lisa Bitel's research revealed that church law of that time required that "the sanctuary of a sacred place must have markers around it."[3] So these great crosses were created to serve as boundary markers, as well as stand at monastery entrances and exits. Residents believed that these crosses provided spiritual and physical protection, and church leaders admonished, "Wherever you find the mark of Christ's cross, do no damage."[4]

Recently my family uncovered our old VHS copy of a favorite movie, "First Knight." I had forgotten how striking the Christian symbolism is in that film—the ramparts of Camelot inscribed with the cross, the great High Cross that stood on a hill "guarding" Camelot, the Celtic Cross emblazoned on King Arthur's armor. This was not merely a superficial nod to a state religion. Arthur governed his land under biblical principles: "In serving each other we become free," reads the carving on the Round Table around which his famous knights held council. It made me think about the usefulness of symbols. Perhaps the purpose of the image of the cross wasn't to alert other kingdoms that Camelot is a Christian city as much as it was to alert Camelot's residents themselves of that fact. The cross around my neck does not serve so much as a proclamation to the world that I am a Christian, but more as a proclamation to me. It reminds me where my allegiance stands.

The high crosses of Ireland are most often "crosses of the Scriptures,"[5] intricately carved with figures and symbols that depict stories from the Bible. One can stand at the foot of the great Monasterboice crosses in Ireland and, with the help of the interpretive literature provided, view scenes from Adam and Eve in the Garden, the sacrifice of Isaac, Daniel in the Lion's Den, and numerous Gospel scenes. It is believed that the crosses were instruments of teaching and ministry; for those who were illiterate and unable to read the Latin Scriptures on their own, the cross served as their Bible. We can just imagine a teaching monk with a group of learners circled around the great cross, some of which were as tall as 20 feet, explaining the truth of God through the use of this incredible visual teaching tool.

The Great Circle

A final feature of the Celtic cross, the one that is perhaps the most distinctive, is the ever-present circle that lies beneath or behind the bars of the cross. It is not known for certain what this circle might symbolize, but there are a variety of educated guesses.

It's entirely possible that its presence was merely practical, serving as support for the great stone arms of the cross. Timothy Joyce suggests that the "circle may represent the sun, a vestige of old Celtic worship, but also a sign of the cosmic Christ, or it may represent a garland of victory for the figure of the victorious Christ."[6] Losack and Rogers point out the possible connection "with pre-Christian sun worship, marking the sign of the cross against the circle of the sun."[7] Amidst these and other worthy hypotheses, I am most enriched by the image of the singular act of redemption laid against the circle of the world, reminding us that the sacrificial life and death of Jesus was sufficient to cover the sins of our entire planet, for time and all eternity.

Another way the high crosses sacramentally served the early Celts was to be visual reminders of the call to prayer. A later hagiography of Patrick states that he stopped and prayed at each cross he met on his travels. An anonymous writer reported in 1693 that "the grounds around the monastery of Iona were marked with 360 stone crosses."[8] Even if that number is greatly exaggerated, half that many would be remarkable for an island only three miles long! If one could scan that earlier landscape, with its great collection of Celtic crosses, we surely would be powerfully reminded of the power of God to redeem all the earth.

Even today the commanding presence of the Celtic high crosses invokes a quiet, meditative response from those who view them, as I have experienced myself when visiting Monasterboice in Ireland or St. Martin's cross on Iona. The combination of its immense size, its placement on the natural landscape, the exquisite artistry seen in the carving, and the powerful symbol of the cross as a redemptive instrument over all of creation draws us into a place of humility, awe, and gratitude.

We can wonder if these faithful artisans, working sacrificially in an attitude of worship as they carved, called to mind their own ancient biblical predecessors who marked the redemptive acts of God with standing stones. "Ebenezer" these stones were called, meaning "stone of help" (1 Sam. 7:12). The victory that God secured for Samson and the Israelites must have been one worthy of history, for not only did it survive through its inclusion in Holy Scripture, but Samuel himself saw to it that neither he nor any of his comrades would forget the way God interceded for them that day. That stone served as a physical reminder of an invisible truth: that no matter how strong the foe, God is stronger yet. The Celtic crosses served in a similar way, also made from stone and purposefully placed to remind us of the redemptive power of God.

Stones of Help

Such sacramental, visual representations of the work of God take many shapes and forms, and are certainly not relegated to the annals of religious history. Each of us, if we stop and take stock, have Ebenezers in our lives. I pass by a personal Ebenezer almost every day, and when I do, I am reminded to pray a prayer of thanksgiving along with Samuel, that "thus far has the Lord helped us" (I Sam. 7:12).

After eight years in pastoral ministry, Cary and I began sensing that it was time to pursue more aggressively what we believed to be God's calling to ministry in Christian higher education. We prayed about this over the course of more than a year, investigating various opportunities that came across our path only to arrive at disappointment when they did not result in a job offer. During this time of vocational restlessness, we also had a growing desire to move closer to family. Our home and roots were in the Pacific Northwest, but our parents and our daughters' grandparents were many states away in Colorado and Arkansas. Our requests of God started to get fairly specific: Lord, lead us to a campus to serve or to a pastoral position closer to family.

During the summer of 1997, Cary's multiple sclerosis suddenly took us down a frightening path. One afternoon he suddenly couldn't throw the softball properly as he and Kelsey played in the back yard. His legs also got numb again. Meanwhile, things became excessively stressful for him at work, and I really began to worry, knowing that stress exacerbates MS symptoms.

When those scary times descend, I find it hard to pray—not because I don't want to or because I don't believe that God will help—but because my heart and mind became immobilized by fear. That summer I turned to Scripture for help in my praying. Our prayers for a new ministry were laid aside, replaced by my chosen prayer for my husband, rooted in the prophet Isaiah:

> *Even youths grow tired and weary,*
> *and young men stumble and fall;*

> *but those who hope in the LORD*
> *will renew their strength.*
>
> *They will soar on wings like eagles;*
> *they will run and not grow weary,*
> *they will walk and not be faint. (Isa. 40: 30-31)*

We went ahead with our plans for a family vacation on the Oregon Coast, thinking that the "down time" would do Cary good. But as we drove southward, Cary quietly announced to me that the vision in his right eye was growing dimmer and dimmer by the hour. I remember so vividly the tremendous weight that landed on my chest as I drove those scenic roads. I had thought we were driving towards light and relief and rest; now it seemed that our road was leading us to a darker place.

That day we arrived at the lovely vacation home our friends had offered us for the week, relieved to meet Cary's parents there who had driven from Arkansas to enjoy our vacation with us. In the days to come we would seek medical help in nearby Lincoln City, and thankfully, Cary's vision would return in time. But it was in the midst of it all that Cary's father let us know that the assistant campus pastor at John Brown University had resigned, and that he had heard they were hoping to hire a woman for that position.

Despite having assumed that any new job opportunities arising would be for Cary, I arrived on campus a month later for *my* interview, and the next day received the offer for my current position. Simultaneously Cary was offered an adjunct teaching position, which meant he would get to do what he always hoped to do, but at a slower pace to allow for his recovery from the recent MS bout.

That day as I walked across campus I passed a statue of an eagle that had been specially commissioned for the university. "Renewed Strength" is its title, with reference to my prayer passage in Isaiah 40. I knew at that moment that God was answering many prayers for us: for ministry on a college campus, for closer proximity to family, and for renewed strength for Cary. That statue, like the Celtic high crosses, serves as a constant reminder to me—even now, almost 10 years later—of the redemptive power of God.

The Celtic Knot

As a culture, the Celts had their own unique expression of art. As Ireland and the British Isles became more and more converted to Christianity, that artistic bent came to celebrate the truth in colorful, celebratory ways. One of the distinctives of Celtic art can be seen within the design of the high crosses: the unending, spiraling, woven cords of the Celtic knot.

Whether we see this knotwork on the Celtic cross, or on the pages of the brilliantly crafted *Book of Kells* (to be discussed in further detail in the next chapter), Celtic knotwork is an amazing, visual representation of what we know about the Celtic faith. Traditionally, the three-ringed Celtic knot that is prevalent in Celtic religious art represents their fierce commitment to the doctrine of the Trinity. Over the years, many have speculated on what other knots might specifically mean. However, there isn't any reliable evidence that each knot had a particular meaning. Aside from the Trinity knot, we're left to rely on our own imaginations.

Still, this incredible art work serves its sacramental purpose as a visible symbol of an invisible truth. Michael Mitton, author of *Restoring the Woven Cord: Strands of Celtic Christianity for the Church Today*, gives his interpretation: "These patterns clearly depict the Celts' love of wholeness and say something very important to the church today about how these people lived their Christian lives. They had discovered the many different strands for our faith and wove them together in a most effective cord for ministry and mission."[9] Certainly the Celtic knot, with its apparent lack of beginning or end, speaks to us of God himself, the Alpha and Omega, "who was, and is, and is to come" (Rev. 4:8)—never beginning, never ending. Such a Being is difficult for our finite minds to grasp. Yet here in the knot we see a strand that moves on an eternal path. Such a path is offered to us as well, for through Christ we enter into that eternal pattern that will never end. "He is before all things," the Apostle Paul tells us, "and in him all things hold together" (Col. 1:17).

J. Phillip Newell is an author who once was the warden of the Iona Community. In his book *Celtic Prayers from Iona,* he writes that Celtic knotwork suggests that "the life of heaven is inseparably woven into the life of earth."[10] Perhaps when studying these fabulous works of art we can simultaneously meditate upon the words of Jesus that remind us of this truth: "Once, having been asked by the Pharisees when the kingdom of God would come, Jesus replied, 'The kingdom of God does not come with your careful observation, nor will people say, "Here it is," or "There it is," because the kingdom of God is within you'" (Luke 17:20-21).

For me, the Celtic knot speaks most effectively to the monastic philosophy that we discussed in our chapter on "Praying the Ordinary": the intentional back-and-forth rhythm of work and prayer, which is ultimately translated as a life of unceasing prayer. The early Christian Celts have given us a marvelous picture of a life in which all activity is considered sacred, that we are constantly surrounded by Christ in every place, and that "prayer should be cast wide"[11] as the Irish tradition states. The in-and-out-and-endless weave of the Celtic knot reminds me that life cannot be categorized into sacred and secular, but that the Spirit of God moves with me through it all, inviting me to prayerful collaboration as we go.

I remember a time when a Celtic knot became sacramental to me. It was Sunday morning in Dublin, and we accompanied our group of college students to the morning eucharistic service at a Church of Ireland just down the road from where we were staying. I was a bit concerned, knowing that most of our students would be unfamiliar with the liturgy; they would have the two-fold challenge of following an unfamiliar Prayer Book and a vicar who had a challenging Dublin accent! Yet the local congregants were exceedingly kind and helped us along the way.

The time came for us to go forward to receive the Eucharist. I knelt on the ornately stitched kneelers and raised my hands and face to look at the vicar as he placed the bread in my hand. There on his green stole was an embroidered Celtic knot—the Trinity knot. I strongly sensed just then that I was partaking of something that drew me into a deeper, unending fellowship: with the Trinity itself, and with all Christians everywhere, past and present, who have celebrated the Lord's Supper. I knew I was part of the unending knot, drawn in even closer by the bread and the wine.

The Role of Saints

For those of us from a distinctly evangelical tradition, there is at least one potentially difficult aspect of Celtic Christian faith. That is the hallowing of "saints," which was, without a doubt, a prominent part of their faith. We can't ignore this, and shouldn't—for though there may be doctrinal issues that we would not agree upon, there are vital truths that we can heartily support.

We've already met some of the Irish saints, most prominently Patrick (who was most definitely not Irish by birth, but who so closely identified with the Irish through his ministry that he insisted upon being considered truly "Irish") and Columba. They, along with Brigid of Kildare (abbess of the monastic settlement at Kildare, Ireland), are considered the three great saints of Ireland. But there are many others we've mentioned— Ciaran of Clonmacnoise, Kevin of Glendalough, Brendan the Navigator, Columbanus, Comgall of Bangor. These are but a fraction of the over 2,000 Irish saints named in historical documents,[12] giving Ireland its reputation as "the Isle of Saints." Some calculations show that "more saints apparently lived on that small island in two centuries than in the rest of the world in the entire period since."[13]

It is true that the Christian Celts held their saints in highest esteem. We can read about the lives of saints through the works of their hagiographers, which, as we've mentioned elsewhere, are greatly exaggerated, yet betray a true desire to preserve the saints' holiness in the annals of history. Patrick's own words, written in his *Confessions*—the only autobiography of a Celtic saint available to us—reveal a genuinely humble man, one aware of his shortcomings and the difficulties of ministering in the pagan territory of Ireland. Yet in the centuries following his death, it is his hagiographers who took great pains to preserve his memory in ways that, at times, seem rather outrageous.[14] A very human servant of God is somehow transformed over time into a sort of Celtic Superman.

It would be easy for us to criticize this type of exaggeration. Did Columba *really* confront the Loch Ness monster as his autobiographer states? Did Brendan and his monks really confront Judas Iscariot? Was Brigid really able to hang her coat on a sunbeam?[15] Ian Bradley provides an intriguing hypothesis as to why the lives of these saints were so inflated in the centuries after their deaths. He explains how it provides a commentary on our contemporary approach to "celebrity":

> The medieval mindset . . . is so different from ours that it takes a quantum leap of imagination to begin to understand it. The *Vitae Sanctorum* which celebrated and idolized such figures as Brigit, Patrick, Columba and Aidan in ways that we find so difficult to take seriously exemplify an approach to the lives and character of the famous which is the exact opposite of that adopted by both popular journalists and serious biographers in our own age. In a culture such as ours where no opportunity is missed to denigrate and bring down the reputations of the dead as well as the living, and the search is relentless to expose feet of clay and find skeletons in every cupboard, it is hard to comprehend an attitude of hero-worship and devotion which sought to build up reputations rather than destroy them. Some of the motives which underlay the production of the saints' lives may have been self-seeking, but they were written to point a moral, provide an example and give encouragement to the faithful. . . .[16]

The role of Heroes is to encourage us.

This modern tendency to tear down rather than build up is worth pondering. And conversely, when we do put celebrities on "pedestals," do those celebrities exhibit the kind of life that is truly worth honoring and holding up as an example? The Celtic saints were honored because of their true and demonstrated sanctity. Lisa Bitel offers this helpful guidance:

> The heroes of hagiography were identifiable by their standard virtues and holy powers. They were missionaries and confessors, not the vulnerable martyrs of the Continent. 'Now

there are three kinds of martyrdom,' wrote a seventh-century Irish scholar, 'white martyrdom, and green martyrdom, and red martyrdom.' By this he meant renunciation of the secular world, penance and self-mortification, and death. While the Irish saints never achieved red martyrdom, they excelled at the other two. Many were missionaries to the pagan interior of the island and were renowned for their extreme asceticism. Most of them lived and worked during the sixth and seventh centuries, when there were still converts to be won and room for new churches. All of them built ecclesiastical settlements, and all were bishops, abbots, or abbesses; some, such as Patraic (Patrick), were responsible for the creation of scores of churches and the recruitment of hundreds of monks and nuns. This is what made an Irish saint: He or she was a pioneer on the early Christian frontier.[17]

The Celtic appreciation for holy examples "resembled Hebrew and early Christian views,"[18] and the Apostle Paul, himself regarded as perhaps the greatest of all Christian saints, considered every believer to be worthy of that title. Perhaps one example for us to follow, then, from both the Celtic saints of the British Isles and the earliest Christian saints in apostolic times, is to celebrate the holy examples of those who have gone before, and to challenge each other to respond to that same high calling.

Another reason the Celts had such a fondness for the saints is their great devotion to the believing community, which extends to the community of heaven where saints reside. Hebrews 12:1 says we are surrounded by a "great cloud of witnesses," implying that those who have gone on before us, saints in the truest sense, seem to take interest in us. However, modern Christians differ in our understanding of the current state of those who are dead in Christ (are they alive now, or in a state of "soul sleep"?). Even so, we can agree and give intellectual assent to the fact that one day we will experience a great reunion with those saints, who may —we cannot say for sure, one way or the other—be invisibly present with us even now.

Conclusion

All of life under the purview of the High King of Heaven is much greater and wider and deeper than we can comprehend. This is where a sacramental view can be so helpful. Visual art, like the Celtic high crosses and the knotwork that is so distinctive of the Celts, and stories of the lives of holy men and women, provide "an outward sign of an invisible grace."

My students chuckled recently as I showed them a projected image of that mysterious and intriguing computerized art form patented as "Magic Eye." This was a popular trend about ten years ago (hence, the chuckling—they could remember growing up with these puzzling images). These images require viewers to adjust their focus in a particular way so as to arrive at the three-dimensional image that is mysteriously hidden in its otherwise mottled, nonsensical appearance. The result tended to be one of two things: 1) amazement and delight as we entered a 3-D world, or 2) humiliation and marginalization because we just couldn't "get it."

Sacramental living, particularly as demonstrated by our Celtic Christian ancestors, offers a vehicle by which we can be transported into a more "dimensional" understanding of the Kingdom of God. Through the utilization of earthly images and words we are called to "adjust our focus," to allow these human-made forms to usher us into a greater connection with God. If we are willing to look deeply, and be patient, we may find ourselves amazed and delighted as we enter more deeply into God's domain. May we "have power, together with all the saints, to grasp how wide and long and high and deep is the love of Christ" (Eph. 3:18).

Celtic Blessing

May the cross of the crucifixion tree
    Upon the wounded back of Christ
Deliver me from distress,
    From death and from spells.
The cross of Christ without fault,

All outstretched towards me;
O God, bless to me my lot
    Before my going out.

What harm soever may be therein
    May I not take thence,
For the sake of Christ the guileless,
    For the sake of the King of power.

In name of the King of life,
In name of the Christ of love,
In name of the Holy Spirit,
    The Triune of my strength. [19]

Meditation: 1 Samuel 7:2-13

It was a long time, twenty years in all, that the ark remained at Kiriath Jearim, and all the people of Israel mourned and sought after the LORD. And Samuel said to the whole house of Israel, "If you are returning to the LORD with all your hearts, then rid yourselves of the foreign gods and the Ashtoreths and commit yourselves to the LORD and serve him only, and he will deliver you out of the hand of the Philistines." So the Israelites put away their Baals and Ashtoreths, and served the LORD only.

Then Samuel said, "Assemble all Israel at Mizpah and I will intercede with the LORD for you." When they had assembled at Mizpah, they drew water and poured it out before the LORD. On that day they fasted and there they confessed, "We have sinned against the LORD." And Samuel was leader of Israel at Mizpah.

When the Philistines heard that Israel had assembled at Mizpah, the rulers of the Philistines came up to attack them. And when the Israelites heard of it, they were afraid because of the Philistines. They said to Samuel, "Do not stop crying out to the LORD our God for us, that he may rescue us from the hand of the Philistines." Then Samuel took a suckling lamb and offered it up as a whole burnt offering to the LORD. He cried out to the LORD on Israel's behalf, and the LORD answered him.

While Samuel was sacrificing the burnt offering, the Philistines drew near to engage Israel in battle. But that day the LORD thundered with loud thunder against the Philistines and threw them into such a panic that they were routed before the Israelites. The men of Israel rushed out of Mizpah and pursued the Philistines, slaughtering them along the way to a point below Beth Car.

Then Samuel took a stone and set it up between Mizpah and Shen. He named it Ebenezer, saying, 'Thus far has the LORD helped us." So the Philistines were subdued and did not invade Israelite territory again.

Reflection Questions

1. What are the important symbols of faith in your life? What makes them important to you?

2. What is your reaction when you see a graphic image of a cross displayed on a T-shirt, a tattoo, a bumper sticker, etc? Are there ways you could use even those occasions as sacramental opportunities to connect with God?

3. Who has been a "saint" in your life? What aspects of their life do you most appreciate, and what steps could you take to be open to that kind of holiness in your own life?

4. Pay special attention to the sacramental symbols displayed and celebrated at your own place of worship, particularly the Lord's Supper. How does this encounter with the early Christian Celts help you grow in your understanding of the significance of the sacrament of Communion?

SEVEN

LOVE OF LEARNING

From Darkness to Light

Iona Journal

I'm beginning my day today in the warmth of the yellow sunroom in our quaint hotel. This is pure heaven to me: coffee in my mug that is fresh from the French press; green plants around me, thriving in the sun; cushioned wicker furniture; old books on the shelves; my journal, Bible, and my favorite fountain pen; and windows that look out onto the greenest of lawns, to the whitest of sand, to the most crystalline blue water. And oh yes. ... I'm *alone!* Fortunately, Cary has come to understand that this is nothing personal. His wife is an introvert; there's no getting around it.

As I open the Psalms here this morning it strikes me that I'm part of a long line of psalm-readers that has been on this island at one time or another. I know that the Psalms were an integral part of the lives of the monks who made this their home. I read recently that Columba would rise early from his cell here on Iona, go down to the beach, and recite all 150 of the Psalms by memory. (It's interesting how the word "integral" describes something so essential to existence that it "integrates" life, keeps it together, like pieces of a puzzle. The regular reading of the Psalms gave life "integrity," I suspect.)

I am writing *words* in my journal, and I am reading *words* in my Bible, on a remote Scottish island where words—The Word—were of inestimable value. I look outside to the grassy lawn and wonder, *did a monk once inhabit*

a small cell there? Did he read his precious books by candlelight? Did he walk on
the path just outside these windows to join his brothers for psalms and prayers?

And where on this island was the scriptorium—the snug enclosure
where the brothers used ink similar to the ink that fills my pen to preserve
that precious Word? They not only preserved it, but *illuminated* it, decorating
it with vivid colors and with gold in some of the most amazing examples of
precision and sophistication ever seen. My little scratchings here seem pretty
feeble in comparison, and my "scriptorium" is, I'm certain, considerably light-
er, brighter and more comfortable than the Iona scribes knew.

I think about words and about the Book of Kells, knowing that it was created by the monks here on Iona. I think about how much it meant for me to
see it, the *real thing* in Dublin last year. That "mother-daughter day" Kelsey
and I had together at the end of our Ireland mission trip was one of my best
days ever: a picturesque train ride from Belfast to Dublin (complete with tea
and croissants); a leisurely stroll through the Book of Kells exhibit at Trinity
College; more leisurely strolling through the antiquated books in the Trinity
Long Room; and ending the day with 85,000 other fanatics like us at the U2
concert in the biggest soccer stadium in Europe. The hometown boys ended
their concert and our unforgettable day by singing their signature version of
Psalm 40:

> *"You set my feet upon a rock*
> *And made my footsteps firm.*
> *Many will see, many will see and fear. . . ."*[1]

So today, here on Iona, I smile as I think about how the Holy Spirit of God
has used his Word to unite psalm writers and eighth century Iona scribes
and an American woman and her daughter and the greatest rock band in the
world . . . to himself.

What are the words I should read or hear or sing today?

*"Jesus replied: 'Love the Lord your God with all your heart
and with all your soul and with all your mind.'"*
Matthew 22:37

A t the university where I work in spiritual formation, we have been
talking about this verse all semester, particularly through the chapel
program that I, along with our campus pastor, help design. This is Jesus'
Great Commandment, and we're trying to help students take it seriously, especially the part that Jesus added to the original *Shema* (Deut. 6:5):
that we are to love God with all our *minds*. I think our students find this
a fairly palatable idea—until they are confronted with the realities of their
statistics research project, or their Western Civilization group report, or
their cell biology final. Loving God with my mind seems possible until I'm
confronted with academic subjects that make my brain hurt.

The earliest Celtic Christians in Ireland inherited from their pagan relatives an intense desire to exercise their brains. We discussed earlier how
the Druid, the Bard, was the center of pagan society. Here was the story-
teller, the wisdom-weaver, the dispenser of philosophy, and he passed his
enthusiasm for brain work on to the rest of the community. When the
pagan tribes embraced Christianity, their love for learning was fairly set
ablaze. This new religion was one of story and wisdom and philosophy!
And there was, of course, a great Book that came with it that happened to
claim that thinking was a good idea and that to do so actually pleased the
one God they now were so eager to understand. "That fierce and restless
quality which made the Pagan Irish the terror of Western Europe seems
to have emptied itself into the love of learning and the love of God, and it
is the peculiar distinction of Irish Medieval scholarship and the salvation
of literature in Europe that the one in no way conflicted with the other."[2]
Hugh Graham provides us with helpful context:

> During the sixth, seventh and eighth centuries the greater
> part of Britain and Europe was in a state of turmoil conse-

quent on the barbarian invasion while Ireland escaped the ravages such an invasion entails. During this period of relative domestic peace Ireland was an oasis in the educational desert of Europe; then, if ever, she deserved to be styled "the school of the West, the quiet habitation of sanctity and literature."[3]

Thus Ireland became known as the *Insula Sanctorum et Doctorum*, the "Island of Saints and Scholars,"[4] and it maintained that status for hundreds of years. This island, isolated from the darkness of the Dark Ages, became a veritable greenhouse of learning, sprouting all manner of inquiry and exploration while the cultural storm raged across England and the Continent. Ireland became the university where virtually anyone could come to learn what it was to love the Lord their God with their entire mind. "The Irish welcomed them all gladly," records Bede, the great historian, and "gave them their daily food, and also provided them with books to read and with instruction, without asking for any payment."[5]

The Learning Life of the Celts

To gain appreciation for this great formative movement and the preservation of faith, a brief revisitation of some of the historical particulars will be helpful.

We'll begin with St. Patrick who, after twenty years of nomadic ministry in Ireland, determined that training centers for ministry must be established, for he certainly couldn't meet the spiritual needs of the many new converts on his own. So, in 450 A.D. a training school for ministry was established in Armagh (in what is now Northern Ireland), the "first recorded attempt at the organization of instruction in Christian theology and classical learning in Ireland."[6] One hundred years later a monastery at Clonard (in County Meath, Ireland) prided itself in educating the "Twelve Apostles of Erin," the great Irish missionaries who went forth in all directions and founded a multitude of schools and monasteries throughout the British Isles and Europe.[7] One of the twelve was Columba, whom we know eventually founded the monastic center at Iona—just one of the 90 or more monasteries he founded (37 in Ireland, 53 in Scotland).[8] So we can see how education and spiritual formation became inseparably linked, so much so that "to the Irish mind an illiterate monk was a contradiction in terms."[9] For the early Christian Celts, the danger of ignorance was far greater than any danger posed by possessing too much knowledge.[10]

Historians believe that by 900 A.D. there were at least 168 monastic schools in Ireland alone. Young people, both men and women in some locations, flocked to the Irish monasteries, even from across the sea, seeking a higher learning that integrated faith with knowledge. It is said that the monastic schools at Clonard and Bangor had 3,000 students each,[11] which is incredible, given the relatively small population of early Celtic Ireland.

It would be logical to presume that these monastic schools were similar in curriculum to our modern day seminaries, but that would be inaccurate. These great centers of learning explored all of the academic disciplines—geography, astronomy, philosophy—in addition to their central studies of the Scriptures and theology.[12] Where the Mediterranean monastics of that time tended to shy away from studying the liberal arts, the Celtic mind loved God by realizing "from the start that, if Christianity was true, its truths could not be contradicted by truths from other branches of study; rather that the one would illuminate the others."[13]

The Artistry of the Word

Still, it was the Scriptures that held the central place, whether in worship or in study. Students learned to read the Latin Psalter before entering the schools, and "most of the Celtic saints seem to have had the Psalms committed to memory."[14] Because the printing press would not arrive on the scene until 1440, the scribes who copied these precious manuscripts held a particularly honorable place in the community.[15] Copying holy works was considered an act of devotion as well as a practical task that needed doing.[16]

If the Scriptures were the central book, then the monastic scriptorium was at the central location of the monastic ideal to love God with one's mind. There in the writing room the skilled monks meticulously copied their manuscripts, each scribe taking great pride in their exqui-site calligraphy and illumination of the holy words. It's a challenge for us to imagine what it would have been like to have had to fabricate all of one's own materials, living as we do in a time when any form of artistic medium is so readily available to us. Calfskin was specially prepared for the book's leaves (called "vellum"); quills were made from the feathers of geese or swans or from reeds; inks were made from soot, plants, wood, chalk, even from the bodies of insects.[17] The final work would be bound and painstakingly stitched by hand.

Smaller books were created for everyday use, but the larger, more elaborate of the copied Scriptures were most likely used as the central piece of a worship service. The most famous of these great illuminated manuscripts is the *Book of Kells*, a large-format "codex" of the gospels with its text written in Latin. "Those who have tried to describe it betray almost a sense of disbelief, as though it had emerged from another world," says Bernard Meehan, Keeper of Manscripts at Trinity College Dublin where the original *Book of Kells* is on grand display. It truly is "the most lavishly decorated of a series of gospel manuscripts produced between the sev-enth and ninth centuries, when Irish art and culture flourished at home and in centres of Irish missionary activity overseas."[18]

This great work was created by the monks on Iona in the late eighth century, and it was believed to have been whisked away for safekeeping to the Columban monastery at Kells (hence the name) in what is now eastern Ireland. However, its safety was short lived, and it was stolen by marauders shortly after the new millennium. Miraculously, it was later found buried under sod, and once restored, was placed on display at Trinity College.[19]

Such spectacular works of art are inspiring even if all we were to notice was the artistic expertise. The precision and design is nothing short of phenomenal. Yet in knowing what we now know about the Celts, perhaps we should consider that these fine artistic renditions of the Scriptures may be calling us to be open to God's presence in a new way. A slower way. A way that does not rush over the words of the Word, but lingers over them meditatively. A way that follows the never ending line of a border of Celtic knotwork, reminding us of the eternality of life with God. Or that the journey of faith that has many twists and turns. Or that God is weaving a perfect pattern, though we may not discern it with human eyes.

Faith and Learning

The early Celts inspire me with their hunger for the knowledge of the Lord and in the way they so clearly believed that all truth is God's truth. They saw the glory of God in all the academic disciplines because they knew that if it was true, it was all God's idea. I love how a wise chapel speaker once illustrated to our students that we have no reason to fear knowledge and discovery. He said, "It's not as if we might, out of our own curiosity, bravely pick up a huge rock to see what's underneath . . . only to discover something big enough to eat God! There's nothing under there that can possibly eat God." In other words, we can freely engage the minds that God gave us to ask all of the questions of the world that we dare ask. God knows the answers to each one of them, and there is no discovery or theory that is big enough to overtake him. We need not be afraid.

St. Columban (not to be confused with Columba) declared his firm belief that spirituality and intellect go hand in hand:

> What is best in this world? To do the will of its Maker. What is His will? That we should do what He has ordered, that is, that we should live in righteousness and seek devotedly what is eternal. How do we arrive at this? By study. We must, therefore, study devotedly and righteously. What is our best help in maintaining this study? The intellect, which probes everything, and, finding none of the world's goods in which it can permanently rest, is converted by reason to the one good which is eternal.[20]

Just a few weeks ago, this news report came to my attention:

The discovery of an ancient manuscript in an Irish bog last week has been compared to the discovery of the Dead Sea Scrolls. The 1,000-year-old Psalter, or book of Psalms, was unearthed in bog lands in the midlands by a bulldozer milling peat.

The director of the National Museum of Ireland, Dr. Pat Wallace, said the find was of "staggering importance" and that its survival until now was "a miracle. . . . It testifies to the incredible richness of the Early Christian civilization of this island and to the greatness of ancient Irish civilization," he said. "In my wildest hopes, I could only have dreamed of a discovery as fragile and rare as this."

The artifact comprises extensive fragments of what appear to be an Irish early Christian psalter, written on vellum (calf-skin). The farmer on whose land it was found notified museum staff immediately, and it was brought to the museum's conservation laboratory at Collins Barracks in Dublin by a team of specialists on Friday. Had the farmer not acted so quickly the book could have been destroyed after just a few hours exposure to the elements.

While part of Psalm 83 is legible, the extent to which other psalms or additional texts are preserved will be determined only by painstaking work by a team of experts. It is possible that the manuscript will be put on public display in the museum's early Christian gallery within a couple of years.

Dr. Bernard Meehan, head of manuscripts at Trinity College Dublin, said the find was "sensational. . . . I cannot think of a parallel anywhere. What we have here is a really spectacular, completely unexpected find." Dr. Meehan said he believes the manuscript may date back to 800 A.D., but he is not sure how soon after this it was lost.[21]

I find it intriguing that yet another pointer to the monastic value, *ora et labora*—prayer and work—has emerged. The early monastics saw their learning and their efforts to preserve literacy as acts of worship. This feeds my own passion for the integration of faith and learning, which is clearly a part of what I do in my professional life. But why should this value be confined to "religious establishments"—to monasteries, or seminaries, or Christian colleges? Surely this call to love God with all of our minds is much more pervasive, calling all of us to "think Christianly," regardless of our profession—to see all of life as a great exploration of truth, to see the world through a Divine lens. The fact is, even Jesus *grew* in wisdom (Luke 2:52).

In his book, *The Divine Conspiracy*, Dallas Willard proclaims that Jesus was "the smartest person who ever lived":

> And can we seriously imagine that Jesus could be Lord if he were not smart? If he were divine, would he be dumb? Or uninformed? Once you stop to think about it, how could he be what we take him to be in all other respects and not be the best-informed and most intelligent person of all, the smartest person who ever lived?[22]

We need not be great scholars or academic geniuses to fully engage in this holy enterprise of the love of learning. The revelation of truth is surely one of the thinnest places we can experience, for God himself *is* Truth. May we pursue it together in imitation of Jesus himself, and of those who have faithfully followed him since. And may future generations say of *us* that we were a people who loved God without fear and with all of our minds.

Celtic Blessing

Life be in my speech
Truth in what I say.
The love Christ Jesus gave
Be filling every heart for me.
The love Christ Jesus gave
Be filling me for everyone.[23]

Meditation: Deuteronomy 30:11-20

Now what I am commanding you today is not too difficult for you or be-yond your reach. It is not up in heaven, so that you have to ask, "Who will ascend into heaven to get it and proclaim it to us so we may obey it?" Nor is it beyond the sea, so that you have to ask, "Who will cross the sea to get it and proclaim it to us so we may obey it?" No, the word is very near you; it is in your mouth and in your heart so you may obey it.

See, I set before you today life and prosperity, death and destruction. For I command you today to love the LORD your God, to walk in his ways, and to keep his commands, decrees and laws; then you will live and in-crease, and the LORD your God will bless you in the land you are entering to possess.

But if your heart turns away and you are not obedient, and if you are drawn away to bow down to other gods and worship them, I declare to you this day that you will certainly be destroyed. You will not live long in the land you are crossing the Jordan to enter and possess.

This day I call heaven and earth as witnesses against you that I have set before you life and death, blessings and curses. Now choose life, so that you and your children may live and that you may love the LORD your God, listen to his voice, and hold fast to him. For the LORD is your life, and he will give you many years in the land he swore to give to your fathers, Abraham, Isaac and Jacob.

Reflection Questions

1. How has study of the Word of God had a transforming influence on your life?

2. How has study of other subjects led you to a greater appreciation of God?

3. Many of us are diligent in exercising our bodies. Are there intentional ways you are exercising your mind?

4. When is the last time you enrolled in a class for the purpose of expanding your understanding of who God is and who you are in his kingdom?

CONCLUSION

CONTINUING THE JOURNEY

⤛✦⤜

My first journey out of the country did not happen until I was forty years old. That was the summer that my two daughters and I met Cary in London. He had already been in Manchester for three weeks, working on his doctoral studies at the university there. The plan was for all of us to meet in London for a short holiday before flying together to Belfast. From there we'd lead our first Irish studies trip with university students.

So here I was, completely new to international travel, responsible for getting myself and our two daughters, eleven and five, successfully to London. We did experience one detour, but our flight was otherwise smooth. The next morning we landed at London's Gatwick Airport, somewhat dazed and confused after the overnight flight, but with a sense of satisfaction. We had made it!

Thankfully, we sailed without complication through customs and went on to retrieve our luggage. At that moment I realized that in all of our brilliant planning and preparation for this, we'd overlooked one important factor: we had brought enough luggage to contain everything our family of four needed for five weeks away from home: four large, heavy suitcases, three medium-sized suitcases, three backpacks, and a video camera bag. Cary wouldn't be meeting us until later that day in London.

It became comically clear that it would be up to me and my two small girls to move this ridiculous and unwieldy collection of luggage through the airport to the train that would take us to the city. We had no choice but to soldier on, a bedraggled American woman pushing one luggage cart while pulling another and periodically hollering to her overloaded children, "Stay together!" I'm sure we looked pathetic.

Slowly but surely we moved along until . . . we were confronted with the downward escalator. There was no "lift" (elevator) in sight. Unfortunately, throwing the luggage down the escalator was not an option (though in my desperation I did consider it). We stepped onto the escalator in clumsy determination, children and luggage twisting this way and that. Just then, out of the blue came a Cockney accent: "Can I help you there, luv?" I thought I would cry as this dear English gentleman came to my rescue. If there hadn't been so much luggage between us, he might have been the unwitting recipient of a giant hug from a sweaty American woman.

The journey of faith that we've been talking about in this book is the greatest adventure known to humanity. But it can likewise be awkward, unwieldy, and exhausting at times. We might find ourselves in a spiritually foreign land, hardly recognizing the landscape, frustrated because the voices all around us speak in an unfamiliar dialect. We grow fatigued from trying to live a good Christian life, especially when the earthly rewards for it can seem so very few. At its worst, we feel desperately lost: has our Guide completely left us here to struggle alone?

A few weeks ago I introduced myself to my new class of university students with a very honest remark: God and I hadn't been doing too well. I shared with them the dullness in my heart, the weariness of soul, and as I did, I noted subtle knowing nods around the room. We've *all* been there. But how do we get past this unwanted place? What do we do in the aggravating, lonely stages of the journey?

Our Celtic ancestors invite us to "step out of the wind"[1] as C.S. Lewis says. Slow down. Listen. Drink in the beauty and creativity of God. Watch for God in every place and every face. Find a soul friend who can help. Relax: God is here. These very old instructions are even older than the Celts themselves, for they echo the words of Jesus:

Are you tired? Worn out? Burned out on religion? Come to me. Get away with me and you'll recover your life. I'll show you how to take a real rest. Walk with me and work with me—watch how I do it. Learn the unforced rhythms of grace. I won't lay anything heavy or ill-fitting on you. Keep company with me and you'll learn to live freely and lightly.[2]

This is an invitation I cannot resist—because it is a rough journey, and I have a good bit of baggage to carry. Most times I don't know where I'm going. Sometimes I'm so tired I could cry. Then I hear him say, "Can I help you there, luv?" And I am reminded of the timeless truth that faithful Christians have had to learn over and over, century after century: Christ is beside me, before me, behind me, within me, beneath me, above me. Paul knew this, Patrick knew this, and I know this. It is what gives me courage to continue on the journey.

So onward we go.

A truly good journey! Well does the fair Lord show us a course, a path.[3]

Endnotes

Preface

[1] Michael Mitton, *Restoring the Woven Cord: Strands of Celtic Christianity for the Church Today* (London, UK: Darton, Longman and Todd , 1995), 51.

Introduction

[1] The word "Celtic" is, in its original form, pronounced with a hard "k," as it is taken from the Greek word "keltoi."

[2] Douglas Hyde, as quoted by Esther deWaal, *The Celtic Way of Prayer*, 70.

Chapter One: Thin Places

[1] Timothy Joyce, *Celtic Christianity: A Sacred Tradition, a Vision of Hope* (Maryknoll, NY: Orbis Books, 1998), 17.

[2] Joseph Duffy, *Patrick: In His Own Words* (Dublin: Veritas, 2000), 100.

[3] Ibid., 17, 18.

[4] Ibid., 62.

[5] It is important that we do not give into the fear that these are "new age" concepts threatening to warp our sense of God's omnipresence. We *know*, both biblically and experientially, that God is everywhere, at all places at all times. In fact, we are very pointedly reminded by the psalmist that no matter how hard we may try (and we've all tried at one time or another), we cannot get away from God (Ps. 139).

[6] Not a Celtic term, but my own; if a thin place is where the division between earth and heaven is barely detectable and God is very near, then a thick place would be where connection with God seems impossible because of the nature of our physical and emotional surroundings.

[7] Kenneth C. Stevens, *Iona: Poems* (Edinburgh: Saint Andrew Press, 2000), 18.

[8] Joyce, *Celtic Christianity*, 25.

[9] Brother Lawrence, *The Practice of the Presence of God* (New York, NY: Doubleday, 1977).

[10] Richard Foster and James Bryan Smith, *Devotional Classics* (New York, NY: HarperCollins, 1990), 95.

[11] C. S. Lewis, *Mere Christianity* (New York, NY: HarperCollins, 2001), 198.

[12] Esther deWaal, *The Celtic Way of Prayer: The Recovery of the Religious Imagination* (New York, NY: Doubleday, 1997), 3.

[13] Alexander Carmichael, *Carmina Gadelica* (Edinburgh, UK: Floris Books, 1992), 248.

Chapter Two: *Anamchara*

[1] Edward D. Sellner, *The Celtic Soul Friend* (Notre Dame, IN: Ave Maria Press, 2002), 14.

[2] Ibid.

[3] Ray Simpson, *Soul Friendship: Celtic Insights Into Spiritual Mentoring* (London, UK: Hodder & Stoughton, 1999), 3.

[4] Ibid., 91.

[5] Timothy Joyce, *Celtic Christianity: A Sacred Tradition, a Vision of Hope* (Maryknoll, NY: Orbis Books, 1998), 11-12. Italics mine.

[6] It is wise to remember that these hagiographies, or "Lives" of the saints, were not written as historical documents with regard to complete accuracy of fact, but were filled with truth and legend regarding the saints, both genres being written for the singular purpose of preserving the unique holiness and ministry of each individual saint.

[7] Sellner, *Celtic Soul Friend*, 45.

[8] Skellig Michael is the name of a small island off the southwest coast of Ireland and the home of a 9th century monastic community. It is characterized by its sharply rising landscape of rocky cliffs where ancient monastic huts still stand and are seasonally accessible to tourists and pilgrims.

[9] Sellner, *Celtic Soul Friend*, 217.

[10] Stephen R. Lawhead, *Byzantium* (New York, NY: HarperCollins Publisher, 1996), 24-25.

[11] June Skinner Sawyers, *Quiet Moments with Patrick and the Celtic Saints* (Ann Arbor, MI: Servant Publications, 1999), #120.

[12] P.G. Jestice, *Encyclopedia of Irish Spirituality* (Santa Barbara, CA: ABC-CLIO, 2000), 83.

[13] Esther deWaal, *The Celtic Way of Prayer: The Recovery of the Religious Imagination* (New York, NY: Doubleday, 1999), 133.

[14] Simpson, *Soul Friendship*, 129.

[15] Edward Sellner assures us that the Celtic Christians were well acquainted with the ways of the desert monks, and that these early Christians in Egypt (3rd-5th centuries) had significant influence on the Celtic understanding of soul friendship. Influential literary works about the desert monks would have included the *Life of Antony* by Athanasius (357 A.D.), and the *Life of Paul* by Jerome (376 A.D.) which detailed the soul friendship between two famous desert elders, Antony and Paul of Thebes. Sellner, *Celtic Soul Friend*, 50-51.

[16] Keith Anderson and Randy Reese, *Spiritual Mentoring: A Guide for Seeking and Giving Direction* (Downers Grove, IL: InterVarsity Press, 1999), 179.

[17] Ibid.

[18] Ibid., 180.

[19] Ibid., 19.

[20] Pat Hendricks, "Helping a Directee Grow in Discernment," class notes, Christos Center for Spiritual Formation, January 2007.

[21] Simpson, *Soul Friendship* , 15-16.

[22] Ibid.

[23] Sellner, *Celtic Soul Friend*, 166.

[24] Aelred of Rievaulx was a 12th Century Celt and Cistercian monk who taught and wrote with great wisdom about spiritual friendship.

[25] Anderson and Reese, *Spiritual Mentoring*, 178.

[26] Alexander Carmichael, *Carmina Gadelica* (Edinburgh, UK: Floris Books, 1992), p. 35.

Chapter Three: Prayer

[1] 1 Thessalonians 5:17.

[2] Henri Nouwen, *Spiritual Direction: Wisdom for the Long Walk of Faith* (New York, NY: HarperCollins Publishers, 2006), 61.

[3] Edward D. Sellner, *The Celtic Soul Friend* (Notre Dame, IN: Ave Maria Press, 2002), 65, 66.

[4] Timothy Joyce, *Celtic Christianity: A Sacred Tradition, A Vision of Hope* (Maryknoll, NY: Orbis Books, 1998), 71.

[5] Thomas Cahill, *How the Irish Saved Civilization* (New York, NY: Doubleday, 1995), 116-119.

[6] Alexander Carmichael, *Carmina Gadelica* (Edinburgh, UK: Floris Books, 1992), back cover text.

[7] Edward C. Sellner, *Stories of the Celtic Soul Friends: Their Meaning for Today* (Mahwah, NJ: Paulist Press, 2004), 141.

[8] Ibid.

[9] Thomas Owen Clancy and Gilbert Markus, *Iona: The Earliest Poetry of a Celtic Monastery* (Edinburgh, UK: Edinburgh University Press, 1995), 151.

[10] Loren Wilkinson, "Saving Celtic Christianity," in *Christianity Today*, April, 2000, 84.

[11] Alexander Carmichael, *Carmina Gadelica* (Edinburgh, UK: Floris Books, 1992), 208.

[12] Peter W. Millar, *Iona: Pilgrim Guide* (Norwich, UK: Canterbury Press, 1997), 28.

[13] Ian Bradley, *Celtic Christian Communities: Live the Tradition* (Kelowna, BC: Northstone Publishing, 2000), 64.

[14] Joyce, *Celtic Christianity*, 26.

[15] Esther deWaal, *The Celtic Way of Prayer: The Recovery of the Religious Imagination* (New York, NY: Doubleday, 1997), 75.

[16] Carmichael, *Carmina Gadelica*, 198.

[17] deWaal, *The Celtic Way of Prayer*, 77.

[18] Carmichael, *Carmina Gadelica*, 199.

[19] Ibid., 34.

[20] Ibid., 115.

[21] Ibid., 108.

[22] Ibid., 94.

[23] Bradley, *Celtic Christian Communities*, 127.

[24] Ibid., 59.

[25] Ibid., 60.

[26] Joyce, *Celtic Christianity*, 7.

[27] Ibid.

[28] Carmichael, *Carmina Gadelica*, 256.

[29] Robert J. Woods, *The Spirituality of the Celtic Saints* (Maryknoll, NY: Orbis Books, 2000), 146.

[30] deWaal, *The Celtic Way of Prayer,* ,88.

[31] Bradley, *Celtic Christian Communities,* 61.

[32] Ibid.

[33] Carmichael, *Carmina Gadelica,* 280.

[34] Ibid., 254.

Chapter Four: Pilgrimage

[1] P.G. Jestice, *Encyclopedia of Irish Spirituality* (Santa Barbara, CA: ABC-CLIO, 2000), 277.

[2] Timothy Joyce, *Celtic Christianity: A Sacred Tradition, a Vision of Hope,* (Maryknoll, NY: Orbis Books, 1998), 36.

[3] Cintra Pemberton, *Soulfaring: Celtic Pilgrimage Then and Now* (Harrisburg, PA: Morehouse Publishing, 1999), 30.

[4] Geoffrey Moorhouse, *Sun Dancing* (Orlando, FL: Harcourt Brace & Company, 1997), 184.

[5] Stephen R. Lawhead, *Byzantium* (New York, NY: HarperCollins, 1996), 85.

[6] Pemberton, *Soulfaring,* 28, 29.

[7] A vagrant monk who wandered from one monastery to another.

[8] Ibid., 29.

[9] Alexander Carmichael, *Carmina Gadelica* (Edinburgh, UK: Floris Books, 1992), 248.

[10] Ibid., 221.

[11] Ibid., 220.

[12] Ibid., 243.

[13] Ibid., 229.

[14] Esther deWaal, *The Celtic Way of Prayer: The Recovery of the Religious Imagination* (New York, NY: Doubleday, 1997), 6, 7.

[15] Moorhouse, *Sun Dancing,* 9.

[16] Jestice, *Encyclopedia of Irish Spirituality,* 18.

[17] Ibid.

[18] Ibid.

[19] Marcus Losack and Michael Rodgers, *Glendalough: A Celtic Pilgrimage* (Dublin: Blackrock, 1996), introductory material by Esther deWaal, 9.

[20] Esther deWaal, *Every Earthly Blessing: Rediscovering the Celtic Tradition* (Harrisburg, PA: Morehouse Publishing, 1999), 39, 40.

[21] Thomas Cahill, *How the Irish Saved Civilization* (New York, NY: Doubleday, 1995).

[22] deWaal, *The Celtic Way of Prayer,* 1.

[23] Pemberton, *Soulfaring,* 9.

[24] Ibid., 12.

[25] In the two or three centuries prior to the time of Christ, the Celts were the dominant culture in the known world, specifically Gaul (modern France), Spain, northern Italy, Britain, Ireland, and Galatia (in modern Turkey). The church at Galatia was an indirect product of that influential culture, making it essentially Celtic. See Jestice, *Encyclopedia of Irish Spirituality*, p. 62; and Cahill, *How The Irish Saved Civilization*, p. 79.

[26] Brendan O'Malley, *God at Every Gate: Prayers and Blessings for Pilgrims* (Harrisburg, PA: Morehouse Publishing, 2000), 60.

Chapter Five: Silence and Solitude

[1] Ian Bradley, *Celtic Christian Communities: Live the Tradition* (Kelowna, BC: Northstone Publishing, 2000), 217.

[2] Richard Foster, *Streams of Living Water* (New York, NY: HarperCollins Publishers, 1998), 45.

[3] Ian Bradley, *Celtic Christian Communities: Live the Tradition* (Kelowna, BC: Northstone Publishing, 2000), 17.

[4] Alastair De Wattevile, *The Isle of Iona* (Hampshire, UK: Romsey Fine Art, 1999), 13.

[5] Peter W. Millar, *Iona: Pilgrim Guide* (Norwich, UK: Canterbury Press, 1997), 41.

[6] Michael Mitton, *Restoring the Woven Cord: Strands of Celtic Christianity for the Church Today* (London, UK: Darton, Longman and Todd, Ltd, 1995), 125.

[7] Ibid., 127.

[8] Bradley, *Celtic Christian Communities:*, 17, 18.

[9] Marcus Losack and Michael Rodgers, *Glendalough: A Celtic Pilgrimage* (Dublin: Blackrock Co., 1996), 17.

[10] Ibid., 23.

[11] Ibid., 98.

[12] Ibid.

[13] *The Renovaré Bible* (New York, NY: HarperCollins Publishers, 2005), 2313.

[14] Henri Nouwen, *The Way of the Heart* (New York, NY: HarperCollins Publishers, 1981), 25.

[15] A.A. Milne and E. H. Shepard, *Eeyore's Little Book of Gloom* (London, UK: Egmont Children's Books Limited, 1999).

[16] Henri Nouwen, *The Way of the Heart* (New York, NY: HarperCollins Publishers, 1981), 30.

[17] Foster, *Streams of Living Water*), 57.

[18] Jan Johnson, *When the Soul Listens* (Colorado Springs, CO: NavPress , 1999), 56.

[19] Geoffrey Moorhouse, *Sun Dancing* (Orlando, FL: Harcourt Brace & Company, 1997), 29.

[20] Nouwen, *The Way of the Heart*, 39.

[21] Ibid., 25.

[22] Ibid., 28.

[23] Esther deWaal, *The Celtic Way of Prayer: The Recovery of the Religious Imagination* (New York, NY: Doubleday, 1999), 99, 100.

Chapter Six: Saints and Symbols

[1] Marcus Losack and Michael Rodgers, *Glendalough: A Celtic Pilgrimage* (Dublin: Blackrock Co., 1996), 57.

[2] P.G. Jestice, *Encyclopedia of Irish Spirituality* (Santa Barbara, CA: ABC-CLIO, 2000), 95.

[3] Lisa M. Bitel, *Isle of the Saints: Monastic Settlement and Christian Community in Early Ireland* (Ithaca, NY: Cornell University Press: 1990), 64.

[4] Ibid.

[5] Derek Bryce, *Symbolism of the Celtic Cross* (Felinfach, UK: Llanerch Publishers, 1989), 76.

[6] Timothy Joyce, *Celtic Christianity: A Sacred Tradition, a Vision of Hope*, (Maryknoll, NY: Orbis Books, 1998), 76.

[7] Losack and Rodgers, *Glendalough*, 59.

[8] Jestice, *Encyclopedia of Irish Spirituality*, 96.

[9] Michael Mitton, *Restoring the Woven Cord: Strands of Celtic Christianity for the Church Today* (London, UK: Darton, Longman and Todd, Ltd, 1995), 7.

[10] J. Phillip Newell, *Celtic Prayers from Iona* (Mahwah, NJ: Paulist Press, 1997, 7).

[11] deWaal, *The Celtic Way of Prayer,* 72.

[12] Ibid., 307.

[13] Ian Bradley, *Celtic Christian Communities: Live the Tradition* (Kelowna, BC: Northstone Publishing, 2000), 161.

[14] Ibid., 164.

[15] Richard J. Woods, *The Spirituality of the Celtic Saints* (Maryknoll, NY: Orbis Books, 2000), 68.

[16] Bradley, *Celtic Christian Communities*, 165-166.

[17] Bitel, *Isle of the Saints,* 10.

[18] Woods, *The Spirituality of the Celtic Saints*, 15.

[19] Alexander Carmichael, *Carmina Gadelica* (Edinburgh, UK: Floris Books, 1992), 212.

Chapter Seven: Love of Learning

[1] U2, "40," *War* (Island Records, 1983).

[2] Maude Bluett, *The Celtic Schools of Religious Learning* (Dublin: Association for Promotion of Christian Knowledge, 1932), 4.

[3] Hugh Graham, *The Early Irish Monastic Schools* (Dublin: Talbot Press, 1923), 72.

[4] Edward D. Sellner, *The Celtic Soul Friend* (Notre Dame, IN: Ave Maria Press, 2002), 136.

[5] Ibid., 137.

[6] Graham, *The Early Irish Monastic Schools*, 27.

[7] Ibid., 35.

[8] Ibid., 36.

9 J. Ryan., *Irish Monasticism: Origins and Early Development* (Dublin and Cork: Talbot Press, 1931), 378.

10 Ibid.

11 D.D.C.P. Mould, *Ireland of the Saints* (London, UK: B.T. Batsford, 1953), 53.

12 Ibid., 57.

13 Ibid., 48.

14 Ibid., 69.

15 Graham, *The Early Irish Monastic Schools*, 105.

16 P.G. Jestice, *Encyclopedia of Irish Spirituality* (Santa Barbara, CA: ABC-CLIO, 2000), 314.

17 Bernard Meehan, *The Book of Kells* (London, UK: Thames and Hudson, 1994), 88.

18 Ibid., 9.

19 Jestice, , *Encylopedia of Irish Spirituality*, 36

20 Ryan, *Irish Monasticism*, 331.

21 "1,200-Year-Old Manuscript Found In A Bog" *Irish Examiner,* August 2, 2006.

22 Dallas Willard, *The Divine Conspiracy* (New York, NY: HarperCollins, 1998), 94.

23 J. Phillip Newell, *Celtic Prayers from Iona* (Mahwah, NJ: Paulist Press, 1997), 51.

Conclusion

1 C. S. Lewis, *Mere Christianity* (New York, NY: HarperCollins, 2001), 198.

2 Matthew 11:28-30, *The Message.*

3 Esther deWaal, *The Celtic Way of Prayer: The Recovery of the Religious Imagination* (New York, NY: Doubleday, 1997), 6, 7.

permission
to ponder

BY TRACY BALZER

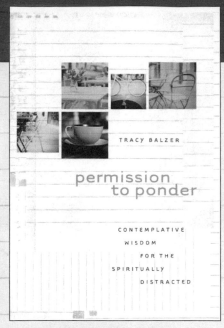

TRACY BALZER

permission
to ponder

CONTEMPLATIVE
WISDOM
FOR THE
SPIRITUALLY
DISTRACTED

ISBN 978-0-89112-405-4 | 176 pages

Permission to Ponder examines the ways others have accepted the invitation from God to dwell deeply, beginning with "The Four Marys" of the Gospels. In the midst of their stories, the classical discipline of *lectio divina*—praying the Scripture—will serve as a template for praying and pondering all of life.

"If you think you're too busy to ponder spiritual life deeply, this book will give you hope and permission to be still and know God."

—**Sara Barton,** Pepperdine University Chaplain and author of *A Woman Called*

LEAFWOOD
PUBLISHERS
an imprint of Abilene Christian University Press

Also Available

Living God's Love
An Invitation to Christian Spirituality

176 pages, $15.99 • ISBN 978-0-9748441-2-1

by Gary Holloway & Earl Lavender

A simple, practical introduction
to the classic spiritual disciplines.
A wonderful tool for study groups,
prayer groups, and classes.

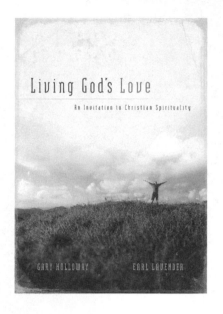

*"Our world is hungry for a life-giving way of life. That is what
Jesus offered—and offers still.* Living God's Love *makes that way
real and alive and accessible to real-world people."*

John Ortberg, author of *The Life You've Always Wanted*

*"At last: a book that brings the essential subject of spiritual formation down
to earth. Clear, reverent, practical, and warm—I'll give this book to people in
my church to help them get on a healthy path of authentic Christian living."*

Brian McLaren, author of *A New Kind of Christian*

Available through your favorite bookstore
Or call toll free 1·877·816·4455

an imprint of Abilene Christian University Press